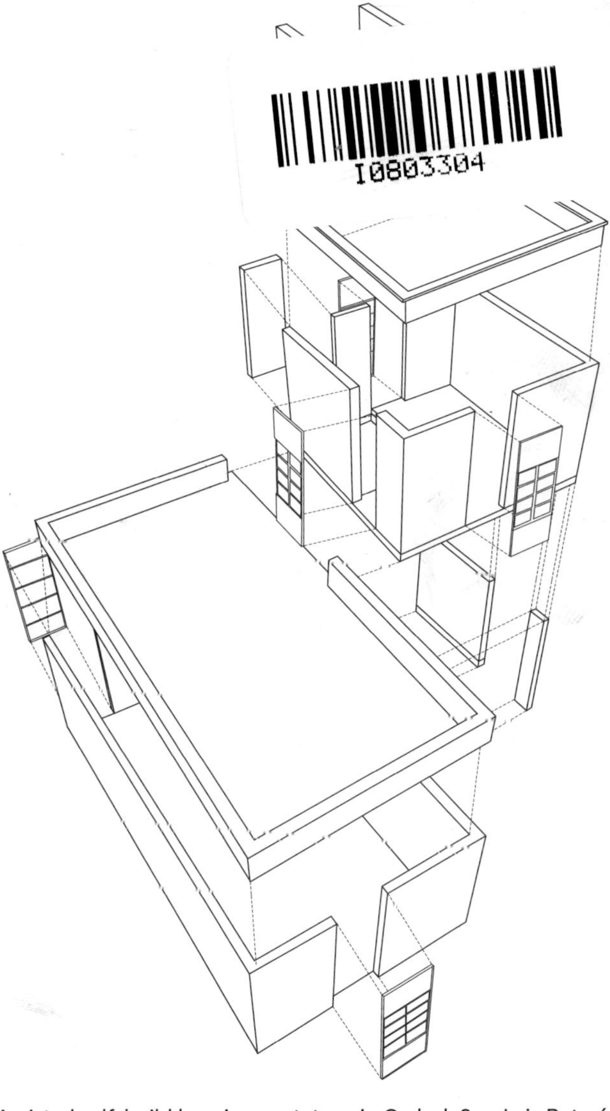

Assisted self-build housing prototype in Cedral, San Luis Potosí. CIDS Infonavit, 2016. Miquel Adrià and Alejandro Polo.

Housing
Strategies for Urban Redensification

First edition, 2023
ISBN 978-607-8880-23-2

Ámsterdam 163 A, Colonia Hipódromo,
06100, Ciudad de México
www.arquine.com

Texts
© Miquel Adrià
© Alejandro Aravena
© Andrea Griborio

Editorial management
Brenda Soto Suárez

Translation and copy editing
Fionn Petch
Quentin Pope

Design and layout
Cristina Paoli · Periferia

This book has been possible due to the support of the Graham Foundation. Its contents have been tested with the students from the Master in Housing of CENTRO University.

Miquel Adrià

Strategies for Urban Redensification

HOUSING

Arquine

6 **THE RELEVANCE OF THE BOOK AS A TOOL**
Alejandro Aravena

10 **1. THE NECESSARY REDENSIFICATION OF COLLECTIVE HOUSING (AND ITS REPRODUCIBILITY)**

16 **2. CASE STUDIES**

24 Weißenhofsiedlung and the advances of early modernism

38 Le Corbusier's Unité d'Habitation: a return trip to Latin America

56 PREVI: Housing as a process
Andrea Griborio

74 Collective participation and a return to the vernacular

86 ELEMENTAL

102 Suburban redensification: recent Mexican case studies

128 Typological transformation and flexibility

150 The Unité d'Habitation revisited: SANAA, OMA, and BIG

170 Recycling

182 **3. KEY CONCEPTS**

186 **IMAGE CREDITS**

191 **BIOS**

The relevance of the book as a tool

Alejandro Aravena

I have known Miquel for over a decade as organizer of the annual MEXTRÓPOLI festival of architecture, and as Director of Arquine. He has a talent for fostering world-class professional discussion, with both theoretical depth and public and political reach.

This is exactly what is needed in the housing sector, and this book shares the same capacity and ambition. This publication may be seen as an attempt to demonstrate that the roots of housing lie in a much larger tradition of modernism, while remaining a constant challenge both for the profession and for society. The idea of addressing the issue through case studies makes it a valuable tool for all those who design social housing, while also making it accessible to wider society, that without question should both aspire to and demand the resulting quality.

Housing, in this regard, is a topic whose importance we must constantly be reminded of. In recent years, we have had cause to hear one recommendation repeatedly: stay home and wash our hands. This may sound reasonable for developed economies, but for most of the world it is a rule impossible to comply with, because of the lack of decent housing and running water. The urgent need for mass social housing has become, quite literally, a matter of life and death. The more knowledge we can share about how to resolve this question, the better prepared we will be to address one of the hardest challenges of our time. This is the reason I consider this book so timely and relevant.

1. The necessary redensification of collective housing (and its reproducibility)

It is generally held that a dense, compact city is more efficient than one that is spread out. Cities grow in size through two mechanisms: densification or expansion; that is, vertically or horizontally. Densification means increasing the built surface area within the existing boundaries of the city, while expansion means adding new areas beyond these boundaries.

If public spaces form voids in the urban fabric and prominent buildings become icons that stand out from it, collective housing is what weaves that fabric. Housing is the lava of our cities. One of the best comparisons is the graph used by Le Corbusier in his lectures, showing how 1,400 residents distributed over 280 single-family dwellings require 3.5 km of streets, drainage, and electrical and gas infrastructure. By contrast, if the same number of people were gathered into one of his Unités d'Habitation, just 150 m of roadway and a similar length of 1.83 m-wide pedestrian walkway on every third floor would be needed.

Over the past century, experiments of this kind were carried out that made housing conglomerations

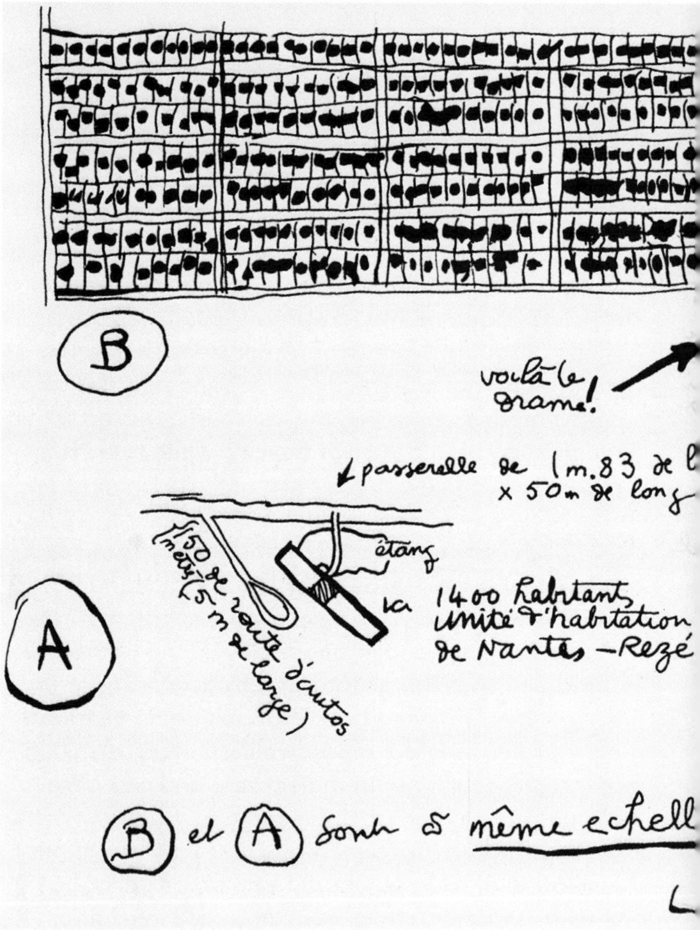
B
voilà le drame!
passerelle de 1m.83 de l
x 50m de long
étang
150 mètres de route d'autos (5 m de large)
1400 habitants
unité d'habitation
de Nantes-Rezé
A
B et A sont à même echell

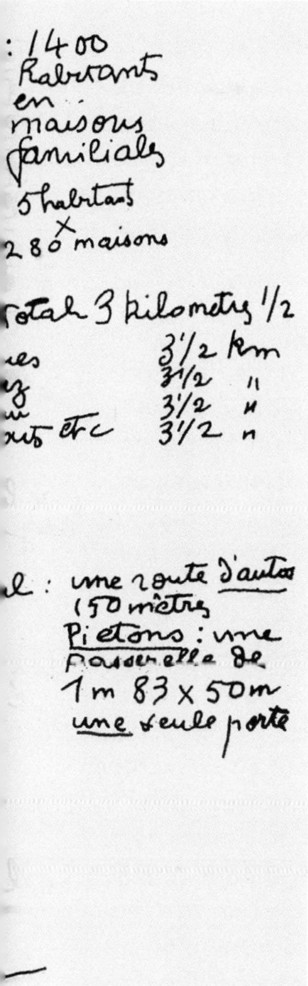

Annotated diagram by Le Corbusier (1957) in which he compares, for the same number of residents, the size of the Ville Radieuse and that of a development of detached houses.

more efficient in their typology and in the dimensions of each area. While in the 1920s and 1930s research was undertaken that laid the foundations of collective housing built all over the world based on stereotypes of model families, by the end of the century and into the new millennium housing types have evolved towards a greater typological, distributive, and functional diversity.

This study explores a range of social housing alternatives that may offer solutions to the demand seen in countries experiencing population growth, and also serve as immediate responses for people who lose their homes in natural disasters, such as the 2017 earthquakes in Mexico. While it is true that there are isolated praiseworthy examples, we must not forget that these are a drop in the ocean given the vast demand for collective housing, both in Mexico and in most developing countries. For this reason, we need to cultivate a storehouse of ideas and proposals that are replicable on a large scale. Recently, Bjarke Ingels remarked that even the most prolific architect will build a few hundred works, certainly no more than a thousand.[1] Architecture, for Ingels, has a great deal of ideological impact, but very little on the production chain, and for this reason he proposed increasing the involvement of architects in mass-production processes, for the direct benefit of society. We can produce industrialized

1 BIG exhibition at the DAC (Danish Center for Architecture), December 2019.

architecture using elements manufactured on a large scale, instead of continuing to produce "made-to-measure" architecture that has little real impact on our cities.

Accepting that the constant expansion of the urban periphery has been a failure and that land is the most valuable and scarce resource in the city, in the territory and—in turn—on the planet, we must manage it for the benefit of society. For this reason, gathered here are proposals that changed the paradigm of collective housing over the course of the past century and up to the present day: projects and experiences that efficiently resolve this problem, as a first step towards offering the best typologies to the real estate market, improving in this way the current obsolete models of social housing.

2. Case studies

Nine examples that propose significant solutions in the field of collective housing and that may be seen in a sense as a watershed in ways of doing things. Paradigmatic case studies that to a large extent inspired or continue to inspire ideas for collective housing as variants on these examples. Considered in chronological order, the case studies allow us to illustrate solutions that are sometimes accumulative and interrelated, and sometimes stand independently. We begin with the Weißenhofsiedlung, a model neighborhood insofar as it seeks a material expression of the earliest modernist notions about rationality, hygiene, insolation and so forth, in the hands of the leading architects of the day. It is neither the largest nor the most radical housing project, yet it brings together singular proposals that make it a true manifesto. Next is Le Corbusier's Unité d'Habitation, an example of a fully autonomous ship run aground, with integrated services and facilities, carefully oriented with regard to the points of the compass while indifferent with regard to the urban character of its context. This is an essential piece in the model of the contemporary metropolis proposed by Le Corbusier, which emphasized open space and independent circulation routes. Many variants followed in its wake, some of them improved versions but also a great number that devalued it to the point of unrecognizability, which regrettably only corroborated the virtues of the original. Latin America in particular was fertile ground for such reproductions of the Le Corbusier Unité.

Also in South America, a singular example emerged to respond to the urgent need for social and collective housing. The PREVI project in Lima not only brought together globally renowned architects of the day (Peruvian, Japanese, British and more) but contributed and drew significant attention to solutions that already existed in some communities in the region. Essentially, this distinguished cast of architects proposes typologies that are capable of evolving over time, starting with basic elements and instructions that enable them to be completed using self-build principles. This is significant in a context where self-built construction remains the most common type, even though—beyond a certain picturesque character that has fascinated so many—it is neither an efficient nor a safe model. As a result, the PREVI proposals brought rationality to the concept of progressive construction, together with formal and typological enhancements. It is true that today it is hard to recognize, precisely because it evolved so much over time—paradoxically a proof of its success.

A consequence of PREVI, and above all of its period, were the proposals of postmodernism and the return to the vernacular, as a certain negation of the universal solutions of the earlier examples, as well as mistrust of technological progress that opened up the socioeconomic gap in society. The incompetence of the institutions and governments needed to bring about large-scale projects that require urban infrastructure—roads, lighting, drainage, etc.—led to a rise in proposals of a fundamentally local character, where the knowledge of the activist architect has a certain influence on the construction processes of rural communities. Guided self-build processes by socially and politically committed architects using limited resources, both local and financial, were proposed as an alternative to the chaotic proliferation of single-family concrete and corrugated tin dwellings.

The proposals by ELEMENTAL draw directly on the lessons learned from PREVI. They acknowledge that the public bodies in charge of creating social housing should be responsible for creating the solid core of the homes, something beyond the capacity of the occupants, while allowing the latter to use their own resources to complete their houses over time. This helps to eliminate the top-down solution of governments across Latin America to sow vast developments of tiny houses on the urban periphery, where they are poorly connected to places of work and incompatible with increases to their built area. The ELEMENTAL model, by contrast, is not only aspirational and adaptable, but generates added value, favoring better locations for the projects. However, unlike PREVI, which placed a lot of trust in the quality of public space and in the generation of community-owned areas, ELEMENTAL makes the assumption that the commons belong to no one and are doomed to failure. As a result, the entire strategy is based on creating the final enclosure for the home with a built nucleus that includes the electrical and sanitary installations. While, as with PREVI, the final result also changes over time, the signs of identity of the original proposal remain, not unlike what Le Corbusier built in the late 1920s at Pessac, Bordeaux.

Precisely as a reaction to the official housing policies of certain countries such as Mexico, where Infonavit (the National Workers' Housing Fund Institute) encouraged endless urban growth with poorly connected, anodyne habitational units made up of tiny single-family dwellings with no capacity for growth, there emerged a number of models that take up many of the previous ideas, focusing on suburban redensification. However, lacking the financial stimulus of official policies, they operate on a smaller scale. Frequently, they are about identifying potential for growth by replacing a self-built single-family dwelling with a small multi-family building. The multiplying effect of a systematic action can radically change a neighborhood or district simply by means of carefully targeted individual actions. The examples developed by Juan

Carral in Cancún, who transformed a marginal district into a desirable destination, or the housing complex by Alberto Kalach in Hermosillo, built by a company that understood the need to stem urban expansion through redensification, are the first seeds of a CIDS (Center for Sustainable Development Research) policy by Infonavit itself, as an alternative to the disastrous previous model.

From a very different perspective, Manuel Gausa's proposals to foster greater potential flexibility and typological transformation are key to the understanding that the collective housing models imagined in the past century no longer apply today. Without necessarily questioning official policies, his typologies (ABC, BARCODE, RAIL, FULL-BACK, etc.) are diagrams of distribution with a temporal aspect that can be adapted to different needs and programs within a single space. Partly drawing on Kahn's concepts of servant and served spaces, these models introduce flexibility to the contemporary understanding of domestic uses and functions, while incorporating the time factor into the definition of habitational units. In his wake, a number of architects have found ways to get around very restrictive European building codes, providing semi-spaces such as mezzanines and closets that can change their purpose over the course of the day.

The next chapter returns to Le Corbusier's Unité d'Habitation, adapted by so many others around the globe. The Unité d'Habitation revisited assembles proposals by the most forward-thinking architects of this century, who in their different ways have given this original model a new twist. It is true that in the 1970s cities and their outskirts, comprising parallel blocks of social housing, offered a desolate vision. Nevertheless, architects like Kazuyo Sejima, Rem Koolhaas, and Bjarke Ingels took Le Corbusier's Unité as a starting point for new explorations in collective housing.

Of no less importance is the example proposed by Lacaton & Vassal to recycle and improve these modern housing blocks, with no need to demolish them: simply updating them. Recycling not only involves renovating heritage buildings but also those of modern districts that have completed their life expectancy and are in a deteriorated condition. Rescuing the public spaces—stolen for use as parking lots—that belong to many such developments, improving accessibility and providing new areas for each housing unit, makes it possible to efficiently and economically transform many blocks originally built on the outskirts and now incorporated into the city.

Nine case studies—the number could be expanded, while some also implicitly contain others—that sketch out different solutions to an issue that remains pressing in most countries around the world. Housing is still a primary need that is insufficiently met for a significant part of the population, and one that demands answers.

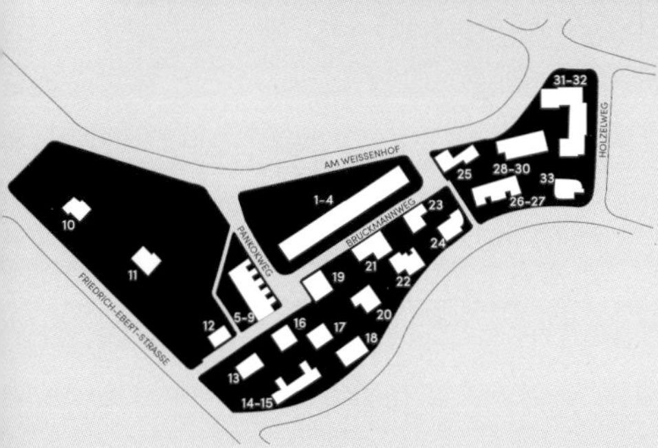

1–4 Mies van der Rohe
5–9 Jacobus Johannes Pieter Oud
10 Victor Bourgeois
11–12 Adolf Gustav Schneck
13–15 Le Corbusier & Pierre Jeanneret
16–17 Walter Gropius
18 Ludwig Hilberseimer
19 Bruno Taut
20 Hans Poelzig
21–22 Richard Döcker
23–24 Max Taut
25 Adolf Rading
26–27 Josef Frank
28–30 Mart Stam
31–32 Peter Behrens
33 Hans Scharoun

The Weißenhofsiedlung was built in 1927 for the construction expo *Die Wohnung* (Housing), organized by the Deutscher Werkbund and financed by the city of Stuttgart. Directed by Ludwig Mies van der Rohe, 17 international architects presented 33 innovative, forward-thinking designs for modern, healthy, affordable, and efficient living. Aerial view (c. 1927) and plan of the projects by the participating architects.

Weißenhofsiedlung and the advances of early modernism

Over the course of the last century, typological solutions to collective housing were explored that particularly focused on social housing. The hygiene and sanitation promoted by the Modern Movement marked a watershed in response to the overcrowding on the outskirts of rapidly growing industrial cities. Ergonomics enabled the minimum required living space to be determined. The experiments fostered by European social democratic governments in the 1920s augured radical transformations in domestic space that took shape on the drawing boards of Mart Stam and J. J. P. Oud, in Holland; Ernst May at the Frankfurt city council department of works together with the research by Margarete Schütte-Lihotzky (creator of the Frankfurt Kitchen); Karl Edmund Ehn, who built the Karl Marx-Hof in socialist Vienna; or the Russian Moisei Ginzburg, creator of the Narkomfin building, forerunner to the cult of Le Corbusier's Unités d'Habitation. Without a doubt, one of the most exemplary and controversial estates built in that period was the Weißenhofsiedlung in Stuttgart, which assembled many of the leading architects of the day, invited by Mies van der Rohe to create a new neighborhood using the canons of the new modernism.

"Mies brought together a remarkable international group of young architects at the Weißenhofsiedlung, an exposition originally conceived as several serpentine terraces of more or less continuous buildings of similar height, following the contours of the site. The version that was later built was changed to an arrangement of freestanding buildings still on the slope and following the contours but discontinuous and of varying heights."[1] The participating architects were Walter Gropius, Le Corbusier, Ludwig Hilberseimer, Bruno and Max Taut, Hans Scharoun, J. J. P. Oud, Mart Stam, Hans Poelzig, Josef Frank, Pierre Jeanneret, Adolf Gustav Schneck, Victor Bourgeois, Richard Döcker and Adolf Rading. In the end, the new neighborhood demonstrated a notable stylistic coherence and established what Henry-Russell Hitchcock would go on to christen the International Style.

The upper, flat part of the site was assigned to Mies' apartment building, the largest and most significant from the perspective of collective housing: three floors of apartments, plus a rooftop service area, ranging from one to three bedrooms, arranged in pairs around four staircases. Of particular note are the ribbon windows on each floor running the length of the building, the flat finish of the façade,

1 *Modern Housing Prototypes*, Harvard University Press, Cambridge (Mass.), 1978, p. 51.

Schwäbischer Kunst-Verlag Hans Boetticher, Weißenhofsiedlung, Arab Village. Original postcard and postcard with photomontage of the Weißenhofsiedlung, Stuttgart, Germany, 1927.

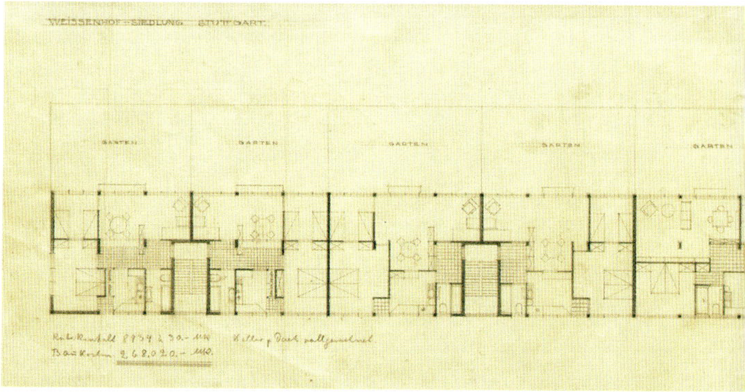

Mies van der Rohe. Weißenhof building.

Top: Façade, 1927.

Bottom: Typical plan, 1926–1927.

and the steel structure. "This apartment building may have been the prototype for the large housing projects that sprang up all over Germany during the 1930s—long, continuous buildings with walk-up units arranged around internal stairs."[2] While some of the architects invited to this collective housing experiment explored their own formal and compositional interests (such as Le Corbusier and Hans Scharoun), others—Mart Stam and J. J. P. Oud for example—proposed terraced housing as an intermediate option between the detached dwelling and Mies' block. Although the Weißenhofsiedlung attracted criticism and mockery for its flat roofs that seemed more suited to a Mediterranean climate, it quickly became a watershed in modern housing design. The social democratic policies of Central European cities facilitated the emergence of numerous social housing districts by talented architects such as Mart Stam with the Siedlung Hellerhof in Frankfurt; Walter Gropius with the Törten housing estate in Dessau; Bruno Taut with the Carl Legien Wohnstadt in Berlin; and Van Eesteren in Rotterdam and Amsterdam. Later, in the 1930s, several of them moved to the Soviet Union to continue working on housing design.

2 Sherwood, op. cit., p. 53.

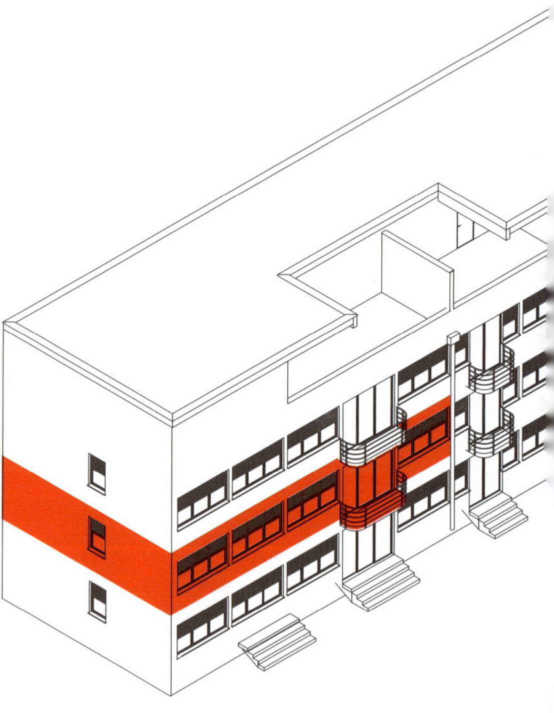

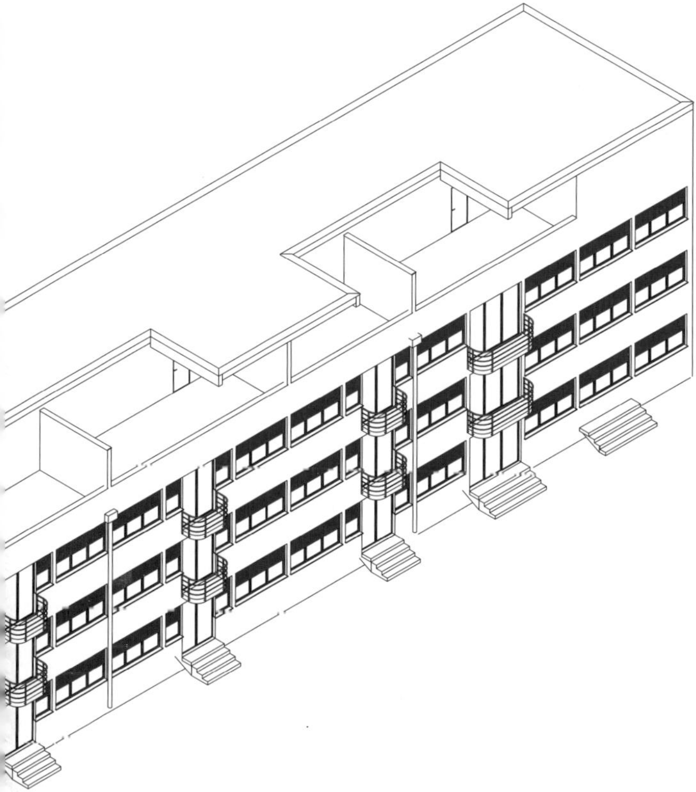

Axonometric view showing the housing unit in the Mies van der Rohe building in the Weißenhofsiedlung.

Top: Aerial view of the Römerstadt estate designed by Ernst May in Frankfurt, Germany.

Bottom: Im Berglehn street on the Römerstadt estate.

Margarete Schütte-Lihotzky. The Frankfurt Kitchen.

Top: Karl Ehn. Karl-Marx-Hof. Vienna, Austria, 1930.

Bottom: Moisei Ginzburg, Ignaty Milinis and engineer Sergei Prokhorov. Rear façade of Narkomfin in Moscow, shortly after completion in 1930.

J. J. P. Oud. Exterior of Hoek van Holland housing scheme, Netherlands, 1927.

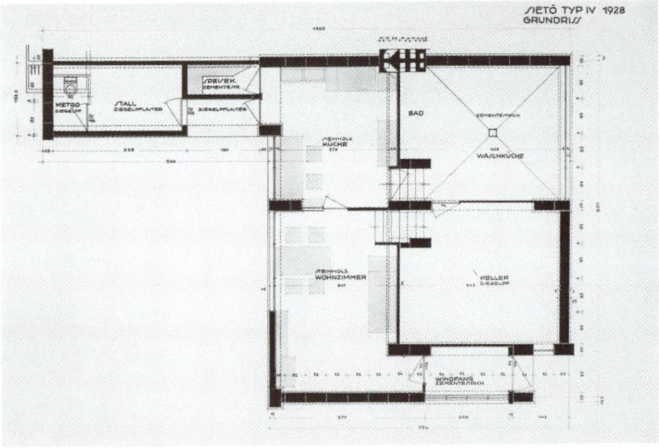

Walter Gropius. Törten housing estate. This was Gropius' first opportunity to put his ideas about the construction of rationalized, standardized houses into practice on a large scale.

Bruno Taut and Franz Hillinger. Wohnstadt Carl Legien, one of the first housing estates for workers in Berlin. Protected by UNESCO for its heritage interest. Berlin, Germany, 1925–1930.

Le Corbusier with his model of the Ville Radieuse, presented in 1924 and published in 1933.

Le Corbusier's Unité d'Habitation: a return trip to Latin America

The Unité d'Habitation is the paradigm of modern collective housing. In many of the urban plans he produced in the 1930s, Le Corbusier was already proposing buildings with thousands of cells for living with all services included. Yet it was not until 1949 that he brought his ideas to fruition with the first Unité in Marseille, before replicating it in other cities. The first modernism wanted to change the world, and the *machine for living* was a key part of this imagined utopia. Without diminishing his individual genius, it is true to say this modernity was doctrinal in character, and the projects seen as prototypes for generic reproduction. In this way Le Corbusier's project was not only repeated by himself, but reproduced all around the world over the following two decades, both in Europe, by close disciples such as Georges Candilis, or the young architects who rebelled against the masters of modernism—above all Team Ten, comprised of Alison and Robert Smithson, Aldo van Eyck and others—and by the Latin American architects who made the modern dream a reality, such as Mario Pani in Mexico, Carlos Raúl Villanueva in Venezuela, and Lúcio Costa and

Top: Georges Candilis, Shadrach Woods, Vladimir Bodiansky and Henri Pirot. Casablanca, Cité Verticale at Carrières Centrales. Casablanca, Morocco, 1952.

Bottom: Alison and Peter Smithson. Robin Hood Gardens, London, United Kingdom, 1972.

Affonso Eduardo Reidy in Brazil, who are some of the most outstanding among a dynasty of excellent architects who built canonical Unités d'Habitation everywhere.

Le Corbusier designed the Immeubles-Villas between 1922-1929, stacking double-height villa-apartments around a courtyard. The prototype of this housing was built as the *L'Esprit Nouveau* pavilion at the International Exhibition of Modern Decorative and Industrial Arts in Paris, in 1925. Taken together they formed a whole city block with public space within and, while this project was never built, it was the starting point for the architect's production over the following three decades until the construction of the first Unité d'Habitation in Marseille. This latter is the synthesis of Le Corbusier's concepts "about the individual family unit, the grouping of units, and the city itself."[3]

A single block oriented east-west on its long sides procures full autonomy for all its inhabitants, by including the services in the center of the building and on the roof. The cross-section "develops from a circulation system of corridors every third floor: access is fromt he corridor into two-level, through apartments that are L-shaped in section and interlock around the corridor."[4] The depth of the façade,

3 Sherwood, ibid., p. 120.

4 Ibid.

with brise-soleils and terraces, protects from the sun from the side, and generates the expressive form of the architecture of this period. Le Corbusier built a further four Unités d'Habitation,[5] but it was above all thanks to his publications that they were reproduced with greater or lesser fidelity around the world.

5 Nantes-Rezé, Briey-en-Forêt, Berlin, Meaux (unbuilt), and Firminy.

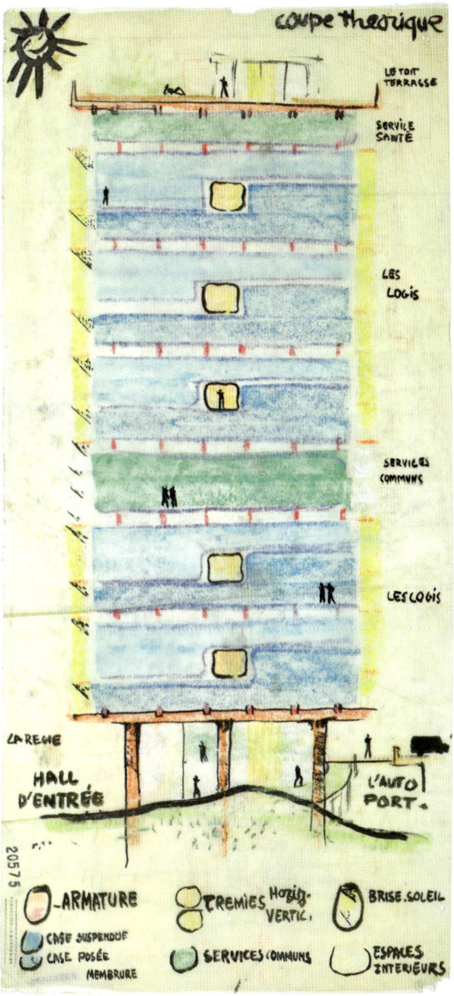

Le Corbusier. *Recherche sur les unités d'habitation*, 1944.

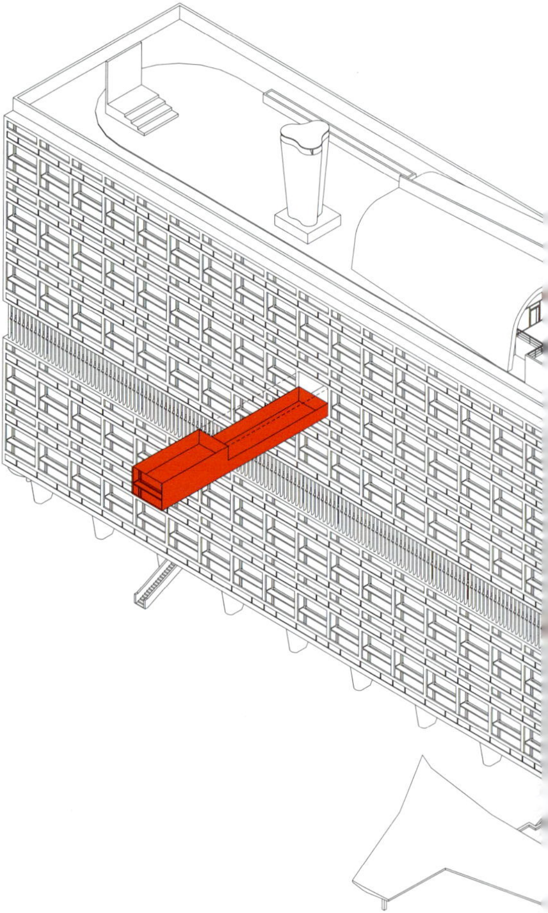

Axonometric view showing the housing unit in Le Corbusier's Unité d'Habitation in Marseille.

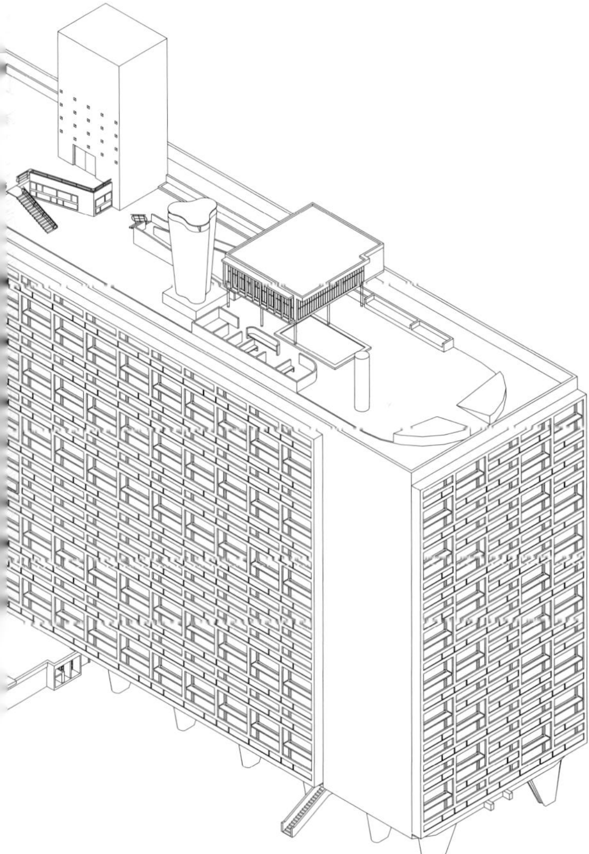

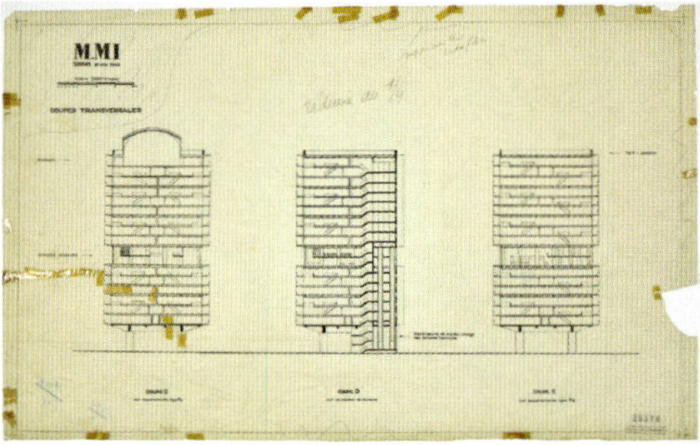

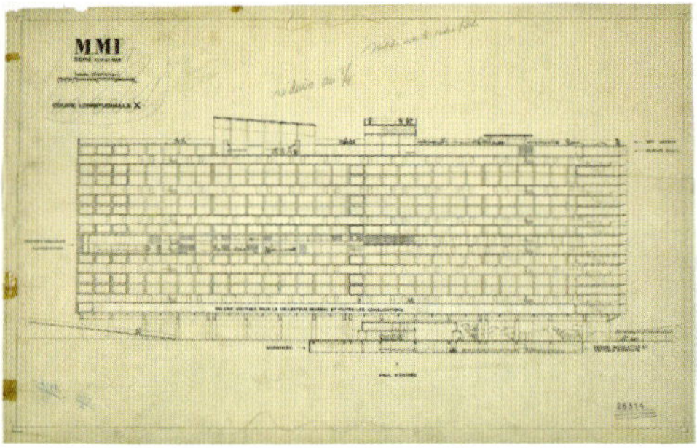

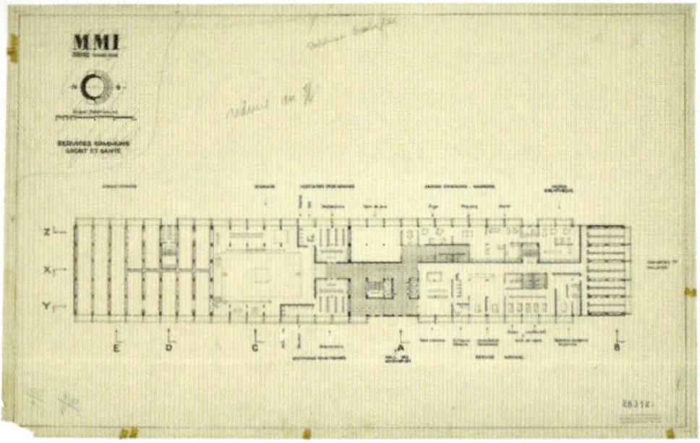

Le Corbusier. Unité d'Habitation, Marseille, 1945.

From top to bottom: cross-section, longitudinal section, and plan of internal street.

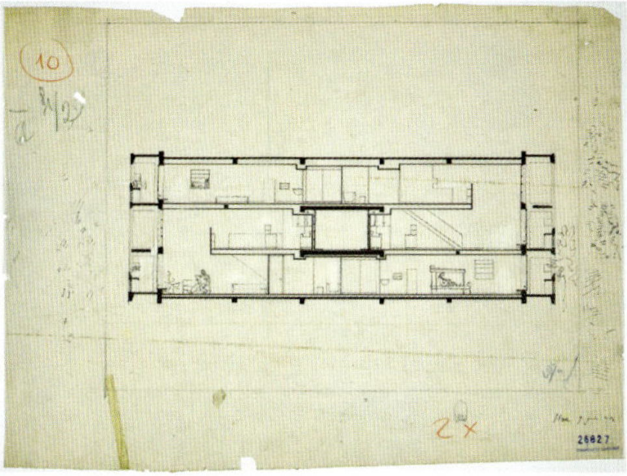

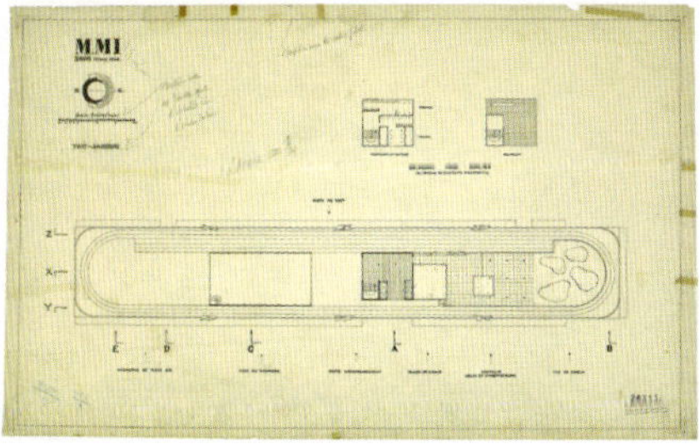

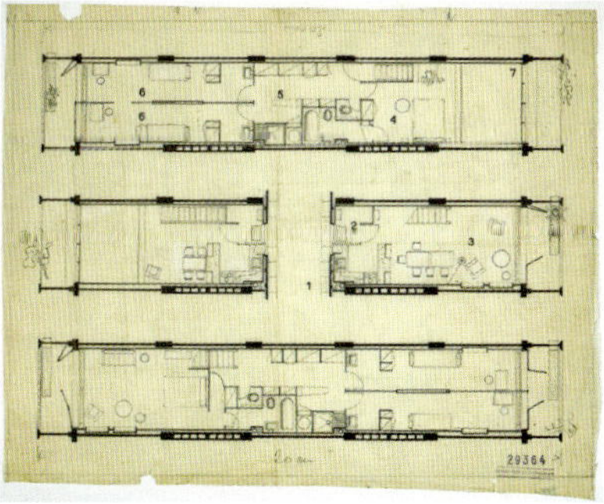

From top to bottom: section, plan of roof terrace and plan of housing unit.

Unité d'Habitation, exteriors.

Teodoro González de León and William Curtis in the internal street of the Unité d'Habitation in Marseille.

Teodoro González de León on the roof terrace of the Unité d'Habitation in Marseille.

Top: Affonso Eduardo Reidy. Pedregulho, Bloque A. Rio de Janeiro, Brazil, 1949-1951.

Bottom: Carlos Raúl Villanueva. Urbanización 23 de Enero. Caracas, Venezuela, 1957.

Top: Mario Pani. Conjunto Urbano Presidente Alemán. Mexico City, 1947.

Bottom: Lúcio Costa. Superblocks. Brasilia, 1950–1959.

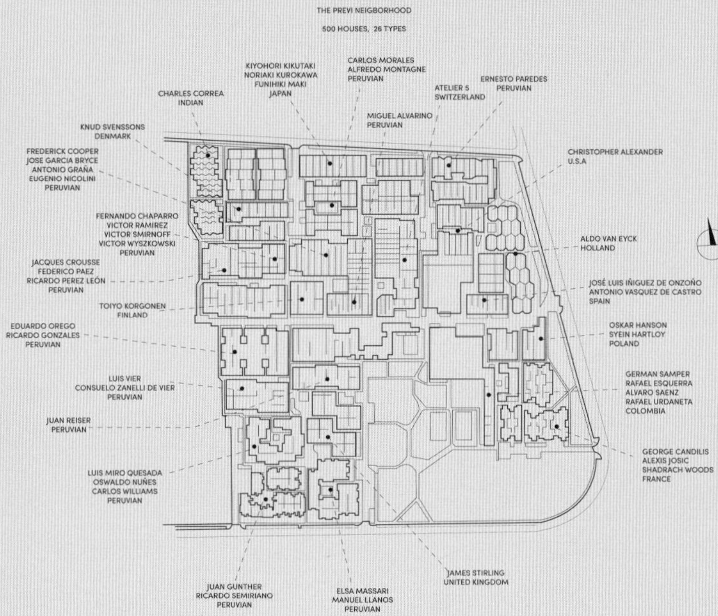

Complex plan showing the location of the housing projects by architects who participated in the Proyecto Experimental de Vivienda (PREVI) in Lima, Peru.

PREVI: Housing as a process

Andrea Griborio

The great lesson of PREVI (Proyecto Experimental de Vivienda, Experimental Housing Project) in Lima is that housing is not only a product of necessity or an asset: housing is an activity, a process that builds community. During the 1970s, Peru had a democratically elected government led by architect Fernando Belaúnde Terry. His term in office focused on major public works, including a number of housing complexes such as the Residencial Matute and the Residencial San Felipe, which reproduced the postulates of modernism imported from Europe to Latin America at a time of great effervescence and development.

It was in this context that President Belaúnde and Peru's Housing Bank chose to partner with the United Nations Development Programme (UNDP) to develop strategies around social housing and urban planning. The lead consultant was British architect Peter Land, who had set up a Pan-American postgraduate study program on urban and regional planning, organized by Yale University and Peru's National University of Engineering, where Belaúnde had been inaugural dean of the School of Architecture.

It is important to provide this political and social context when talking about PREVI, since it is so rare for the political and technical stars to align in such a way that an initiative of this kind can come to fruition. Naturally, knowing the sequence of events, we can understand the outcome of the project. In September 1968 the Operational Plan was signed by the Peruvian government and the UNDP, with Peter Land as project director and liaison between the UN and the government. In 1968, a military coup overthrew Belaúnde and a junta took power. Although the new government reaffirmed its commitment to continue the PREVI project, it installed new people in all the key posts and made alterations that significantly reduced the initial expectations. PREVI was concluded in 1973.

The original project for PREVI comprised three action plans around the theme of social housing, called Pilot Projects (PP). PP1 was to develop a new district of low-cost housing, including shared services with new and improved designs and with special attention to both new and existing construction methods that made the most efficient use of resources. This would be chosen from the results of an international competition, and remains the best-known aspect of PREVI due to the prominent figures who took part and the way it has evolved as a complex. Meanwhile, PP2 consisted of a study for the renovation of housing and communities in areas of the city in decline, the outcome of which was a report delivered to the government with recommendations for implementation. Finally, PP3 was focused on the issue of self-build housing, and produced projects focused on the requirements arising from this need and providing technical assistance for migrants, squatters, and people with few resources. The consequences of the earthquake that struck Lima in 1970 led to this project being split into two: PP3, which continued working on self-build, earthquake-resistant, housing, and PP4, which focused on providing housing solutions to those who had lost homes, as part of the reconstructions plans, and with the support and consultancy of the UN.

The Experimental Housing Project in Lima was conceived as an opportunity to understand and build solutions that were targeted, viable, and affordable for the Latin American context. Out of the whole project, the part that has endured is Pilot Project 1, the new district, which was designed in accordance with these premises: low-rise and high-density, with a view to both the module and the model of future urban growth; a human-scale, pedestrian context with a neighborhood-level landscaping and an earthquake-proof building method that allowed for rationalization and industrialization of construction processes. The housing type had to be treated as a flexible space that allowed for progressive growth, based on the use of construction systems that, rather than implementing costly, industrialized mechanisms, increased the use of labor, improving techniques and introducing new and more practical models.

Peter Land selected the international architects invited to take part in the 1969 competition, choosing the studios he considered best-qualified to identify thoughtful solutions to the housing issue, weighted for geographic quotas and considering the talent and experience from both developed and developing countries. In turn, an open competition was organized for Peruvian architects, in order to ensure there were as many local proposals as there were international ones. Both foreign and Peruvian teams had to follow the same rules and timescales. They were not necessarily star architects; it was a bonus to have worked on low-rise and high-density housing, as the realist, new alternative to the challenge set out by the competition. An example of this is the selection of Germán Samper and his team, who in 1958 had developed the La Fragua neighborhood in Bogotá, where they explored the typology of the flexible, expandable housing that also offered the possibility of productive activities. Equally, there were the exercises of Georges Candilis and Shadrach Woods, who had developed a number of low-cost housing projects in North Africa at their ATBAT studio, and already contravened several modernist principles in their determination to find a progressive, human-scale architecture. It is interesting to note that both Samper and Candilis had been close disciples of Le Corbusier, and played an active part in the Congrès Internationaux d'Architecture Moderne (CIAM) debates, contributing to reflection on the successes and failures of their teacher's modernist ideas.

The international contestants were: Herbert Ohl from Germany (awarded, unbuilt); James Stirling from England; Knud Svenssons from Denmark; Rafael Esguerra; Alvaro Saenz; Rafael Urdaneta and Germán Samper from Colombia; Atelier 5 from Switzerland (awarded); Toivo Korhonen from Finland; Charles Correa from India; Fumihiko Maki; Kisho Kurokawa and Kiyonori Kikutake from Japan (awarded); José Luis Íñiguez de Onzoño and Antonio Vázquez de Castro from Spain; Oskar Hansen and Svein Hatløy from Poland; Aldo van Eyck from the Netherlands; Georges Candilis, Alexis Josic and Shadrach Woods from France and the Center for Environmental Structure (Christopher Alexander) from the United States. The Peruvians Miguel Alvariño; Ernesto Paredes; Luis Miro Quesada; Carlos Williams and Oswaldo Núñez; Juan Gunter and Mario Seminario; Carlos Morales and Eugenio Montagne; Juan Reiser; Eduardo Orrego; Luis Vier and Consuelo Zanelli (unbuilt); Franco Vella, José Bentín, Raúl Quiñones and Luis Takahashi; Elsa Mazzari and Manuel Llanos (awarded); Frederick Cooper, José García-Bryce, Antonio Graña and Eugenio Nicolini; Fernando Chaparro, Víctor Ramírez, Víctor Smirnoff and Víctor Wiskowsky (awarded); Jacques Crousse, Jorge Páez and Ricardo Pérez-León (awarded).

An international jury comprising José Antonio Coderch (Spain); Halldør Gunnlogsson (Denmark); Peter Land and Ernest Weissmann (for the UN); Carl Koch (USA and IAU); Manuel Valega, Ricardo Malachowski and Eduardo Barclay (Peru) met in Lima in August 1969 and, having awarded six cash prizes (three international and three local) announced that, given the high quality of the entries, a small cluster of each of the proposals would be constructed, with the aim of taking advantage of each.

In the end, 500 homes were built instead of the 1,500 originally intended. Contracts were signed with the 26 entrants to develop their respective projects; they had to work with engineers, and each proposal was required to include the final model house and a cluster of about 20 units. The houses were to include phased growth units: a basic one-story unit and up to two or three growth units. In turn, a completed unit was to serve as an example in each cluster, as a model to be followed for future expansion of the rest.

Next, the overall plan of the PREVI was developed by Peter Land together with a mixed group of international and Peruvian specialists in different fields. The plan for the new neighborhood included a school, kindergarten, stores, administrative area, health clinic, and neighborhood center strategically located to serve a growing community. The layout of the new district classified circulation routes by scale and assigned vehicular traffic to the perimeter, with secondary roads leading to key centers and collective parking areas. Meanwhile, PREVI implemented a network of pedestrian routes on two scales connecting the different plazas and intersection nodes between the housing clusters, together with a central pedestrian esplanade that gives direction to the neighborhood and a human-scale identity.

PREVI represented a call for rationalization in construction and expansion over time. It aimed to be a project with innovative technology, taking the compact, private home as the basic platform for a high-density neighborhood. As a result, from the outset the competition encouraged flexibility in design and the use of technologies capable of adapting to future alterations. The proposals received include a huge variety of construction solutions, some using heavy industry processes, some simple *in situ* prefabrication with a clear construction logic, and others merely a rationalization of traditional building processes. Due to the technical challenges involved, two of the projects were not built: that of Herbert Ohl from Germany, and that of Luis Vier and Consuelo Zanelli, a Peruvian team.

For Jacques Crousse, a Peruvian participant in the competition, the project evolved into a showcase of prefabrication systems, whose validity became moot since clusters of just 20 houses were built, therefore avoiding the question of recovering their initial implementation costs through repetition on a larger scale. As a result, many of the initial aims of the project lost relevance, and none of the proposed construction systems really had its performance and capability tested. In the end, the only long-term survivors of the industrialization proposal were the

PREVI brick—a basic construction element—and a prefabricated spiral staircase.

In any case, the initial plan was never fully carried out. The intention was that the homes that were best received would be reproduced, and an adjacent site had even been acquired for this purpose. In time, this land was ceded for other services, and self-built housing appeared there. However, some of the planned infrastructure, such as the neighborhood center and the school, failed to materialize. Nor did the idea of turning the project's own offices and workshops into a support center for maintenance of the homes and providing advice to residents seeking to expand them. As a result, the project and its occupants were left abandoned, without the spatial and construction guide intended by the architects, something that would doubtless have helped to preserve a certain visual continuity and ensure the structural security of the extensions.

At a time when the global trend in social housing was towards the vertical, PREVI represented a vote for the advantages of low-rise density, considering the benefits in terms of access, human scale, privacy, maintenance, property, and above all the possibility of expansion in response to changes in family size over time. Even though the resulting extensions to many of the homes do not appear to have followed either the original design or the structural principles, and many of the distinguishing characteristics that identified the original projects by renowned architects have been lost, in PREVI there still prevails the idea of a living, complex city, where a diversification of uses and styles has appeared spontaneously, transforming it into an active, flexible neighborhood that is integrated organically into the city, its origin blurred. Almost half a century later, PREVI is a fully constituted neighborhood that is full of possibilities, an example that we should examine with care to understand its successes and failures, and without doubt the most important forerunner in Latin America in terms of progressive, low-rise, high-density housing.

PREVI is the result of a process that began with recognizing the universal importance of housing, combined with the contribution of users as a trigger for making city, an event in itself that continues to do honor to its experimental character. It is one where the idea of an open, malleable, changing, and culture-rich city endures. A project that values the house as a process, where the open and undefined comes before the limited and completed, and where the occupant is the one who instills value in the property and the city through time and through their direct participation.

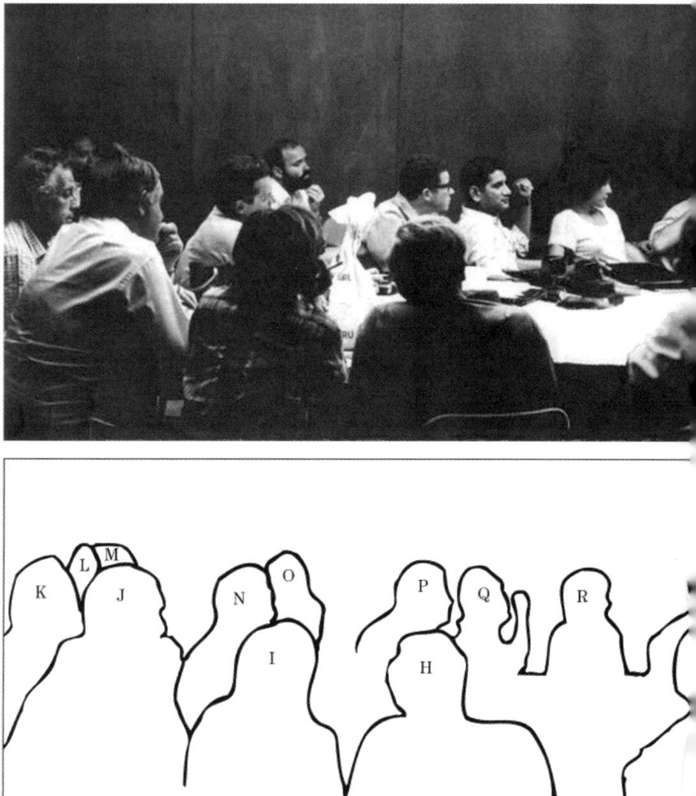

Field trip to Lima. Briefing session with international architects at the Housing Bank (Lima) with Peter Land, director of the UN PREVI project.

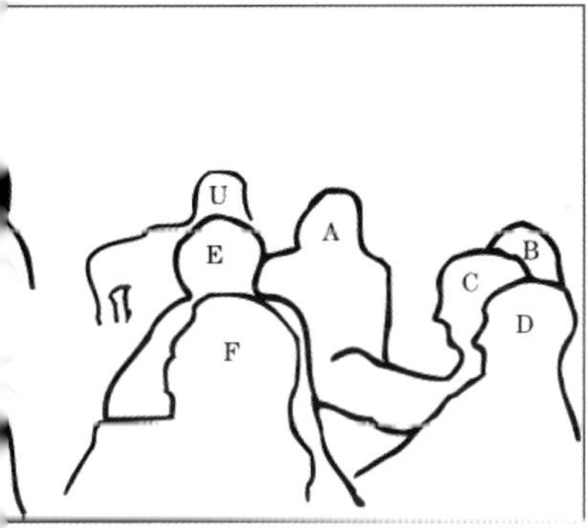

A. Peter Land, UN Project Manager, United Kingdom.

B. José Luis Íñiquez de Ozoño, Spain.

C. Alfredo Pini (Atelier 5), Switzerland.

D. Anatole Du Fresne (Atelier 5).

E. Toivo Korhonen, Finland.

F. Knud Svenssons, Denmark.

G. Oskar Hanson, Poland.

H. Svein Hartloy, Poland.

I. Unidentified person.

J. James Stirling, United Kingdom.

K. Aldo van Eyck, Netherlands.

L. Fumihiko Maki, Japan.

M. Kionori Kikutake, Japan.

N. Alexis Josic (Candilis, Josic and Woods).

O. Antonio Vazquez de Castro, Spain.

P. Germán Samper, Colombia.

Q. Charles Correa, India.

R. Sara Ishikawa, United States.

S. Christopher Alexander, United States.

T. Oscar Pacheco, Co-director of the project, Peru.

U. Álvaro Ortega, UN Advisor.

PREVI. Aerial photograph (1976) and model of the 24 housing typologies that comprise the development.

Prefabricated systems.

James Stirling. Housing prototypes for PREVI, 1978. Aerial view and façade.

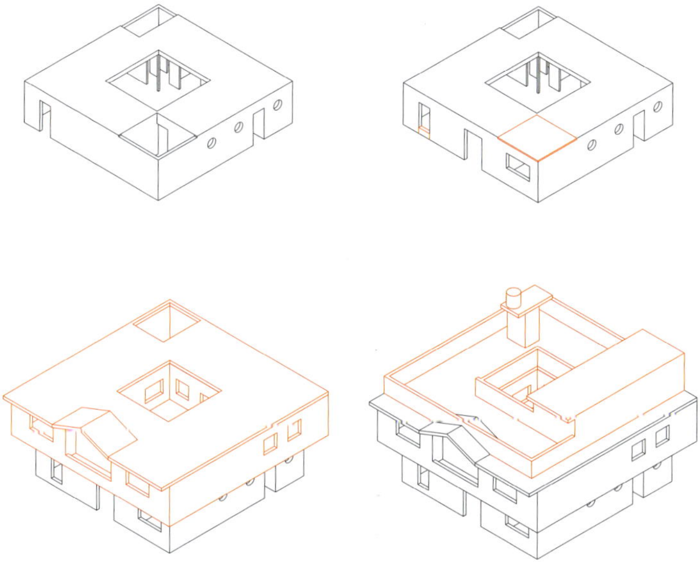

Axonometric view showing the alterations made by the Zamora family, living in one of the PREVI prototypes designed by James Stirling.

Before and after. Alterations made by residents of the PREVI neighborhood.

Protesters gathered at the Plaza de las Tres Culturas, Tlatelolco, October 2, 1968.

Collective participation and a return to the vernacular

In the late 1960s, a series of seismic shifts—the May 1968 events in France, the sexual revolution, the Warsaw Pact invasion of Czechoslovakia, the Tlatelolco massacre in Mexico City, etc.—challenged the postwar model of social order and progress. Architecture was also caught up in these changes. Postmodernity proposed multiple truths instead of a *single truth*, reviving the historical importance of the past given the evident failure of a dehumanized modernity and exploring the roots and local values forgotten by Internationalism. Buffeted by coups and dictatorships, Latin America saw the rise of several architecture collectives eager to return to the principles of social responsibility and to forsake the global technological progress of that era.

In Mexico, social housing was a priority for the postrevolutionary regimes from the early decades of the 1900s. Juan O'Gorman, with his Vivienda obrera de transición and Ciudad obrera projects, proposed social housing that merged the public and social realms.[6] Alberto T. Arai's Casa campesina tropical (1941), as well as the artist-studios of Luis Barragán and Max Cetto (1941), Pedro Ramírez Vázquez's ideas for the Aula-casa rural (1958), and the Casa que crece (1962), were remarkable experiments that took a local perspective on the most radical ideas of modernity. Mario Pani, meanwhile, completed a project on an urban scale: Unidad Modelo (1947, with Félix Sánchez) provided housing units for 15,000 people, inserting public services amid the residential blocks and mass-produced housing developments; shortly afterward, he gave Mexico a Corbusier-type Unité d'habitation with his CUPA housing complex (in 1949, a year before Le Corbusier himself completed his first Unité d'habitation in Marseille), the Benito Juárez housing complex a year later, and finally Nonoalco-Tlatelolco (1964), a city within the city to replace the existing "horseshoe slum" surrounding the city center. Other housing complexes included Félix Sánchez's Unidad Jardín Balbuena (1952), Mario Pani and Salvador Ortega's UH Santa Fe (1957), and UH Independencia (1960) by Alejandro Prieto, José María Gutiérrez, Pedro Miret, Manuel Santiago, Manuel San Román, Carlos Villaseñor, and Leonel Pérez—models that failed to become the standard in a metropolis that was outgrowing all planning initiatives.

6 Canales, Fernanda, *Vivienda colectiva en México. El derecho a la arquitectura,* Editorial GG, Mexico City, 2017, p. 27.

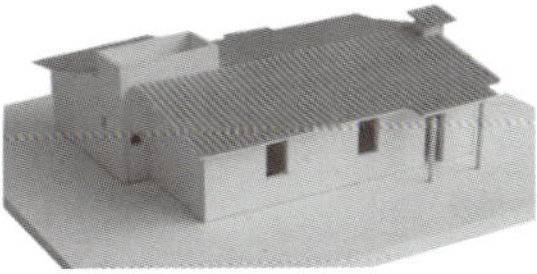

Oscar Hagerman, social housing design in San Andrés Yahuitalpan, Puebla.

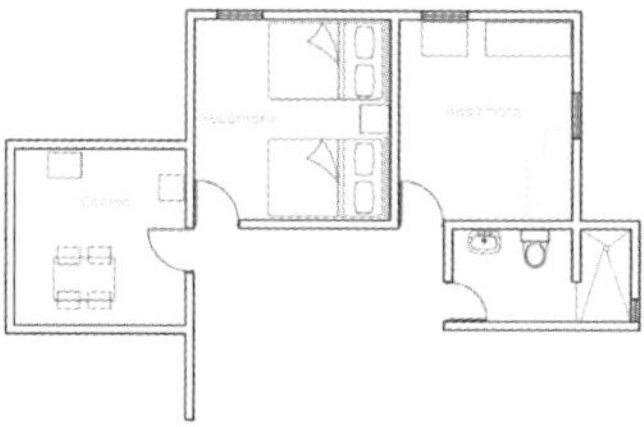

PRIMERA ETAPA

Posibles etapas de crecimiento
en casa tipo
San Andrés Yahuitlalpan
ESC. 1:75

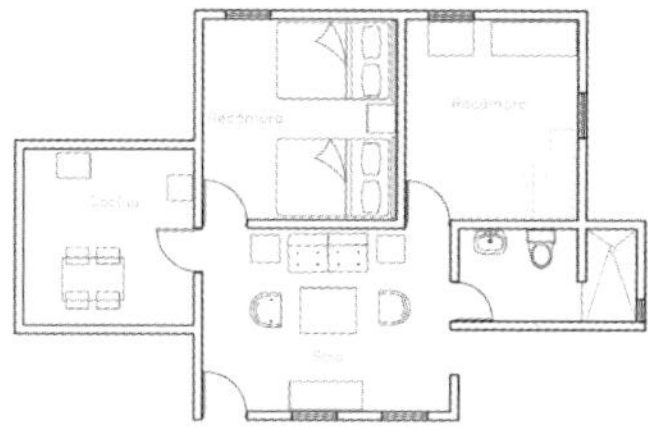

SEGUNDA ETAPA

Posibles etapas de crecimiento
en casa tipo
San Andrés Yahuitlalpan
ESC. 1:75

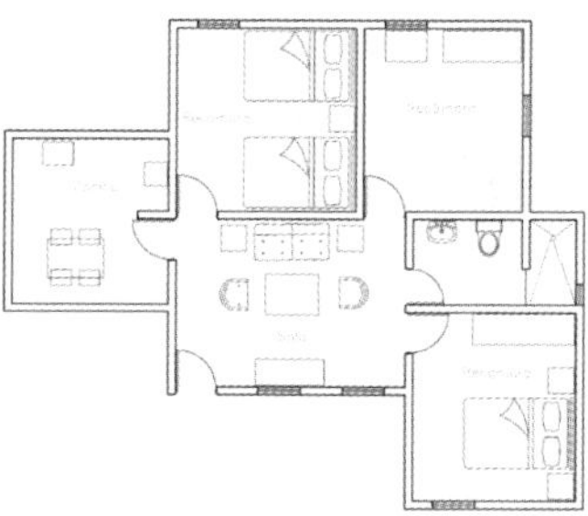

TERCERA ETAPA

Posibles etapas de crecimiento
en casa tipo
San Andrés Yahuitlalpan
ESC. 1:75

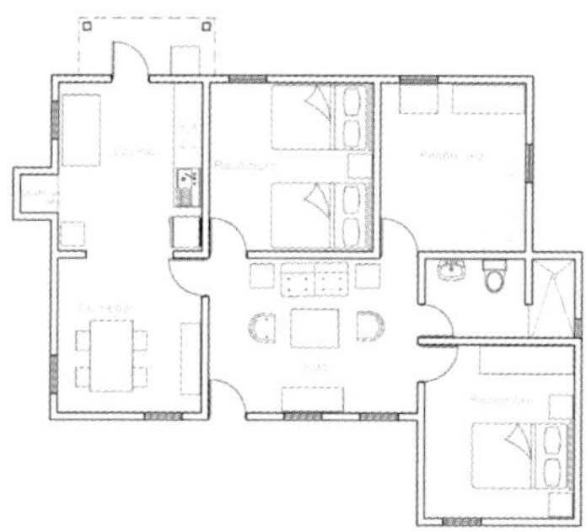

CUARTA ETAPA

Posibles etapas de crecimiento
en casa tipo
San Andrés Yahuitlalpan
ESC. 1:75

Oscar Hagerman, social housing design in San Andrés Yahuitalpan, Puebla. Possible extension phases.

In rural Mexico, "reappraising lessons from the past became a way of life for Oscar Hagerman and Carlos González Lobo. Both saw flexibility as something not just about space but also structure and procedure, and they adapted their work to local processes; their projects incorporate the methods that people use when building themselves, and they grasp local realities." They swapped prefabricated and modular systems using industrialized techniques with a reinterpretation of traditional materials and an acknowledgment of skilled local labor so that—as Hagerman put it himself—"everyone can build what they need and make the most of what they already have."[7]

González Lobo conceived the house as a "vast shed" for users to build and adapt. A light, curving roof creates a large volume buildable by anyone within a few hours; it can even incorporate a second story when the house grows. González Lobo's guiding principle—"maximum space at the lowest cost"—is manifest in the idea of a shell that grows and evolves out of a basic structure. His prototypes build on the lessons of O'Gorman's and Legaretta's functionalist architecture, and on the teachings of his mentor, Antonio Pastrana, who developed the idea of "seed homes" and "removable houses."[8]

7 Ibid., p. 19.

8 Ibid., p. 20.

For Lobo, emergency housing must consist of solutions inherent in popular and self-managed architecture "using *appropriated and appropriable technologies.* First and foremost, technology which, for the same cost, makes it possible to build more square meters: 'maximum space for the lowest cost,' through efficiency achieved by: a) a structural use of cement-foundations, b) reinforced concrete structural reinforcements in 'corner plates' on load-bearing walls, and c) roofs with self-supporting geometrical designs, in addition to construction procedures compatible with self-built housing."[9] His concept of the Vast Shed derives from the idea of offering buildable potential and volume, so that for the cost of a room it is possible to prepare for a two-story building that can grow, in the understanding that an architect "must become involved and participate actively in the social transformation urgently required today."[10] The solution consists of "inflating the house's internal volume, which deforms the roof and offers an arched surface that not only generates extra cubic meters with the same height of wall frame, but also requires less concrete and structural elements due to the geometry, lowering its price."[11] Meanwhile, an inner

9 González Lobo, Carlos. *Academia XXII* · UNAM · ISSN: 2007–252X, first period, year 6, no. 11, Mexico City, May 2015, p. 154.

10 González Ortiz, Humberto. Thesis on Carlos González Lobo, UNAM, 2003, p. 122.

11 Serrano Macías, Andrés, *Vivienda Crecedera. Prototipo para la regeneración urbana en Valle del Paraíso.* BA thesis, Escuela Técnica Superior de Madrid (ETSAM), 2018.

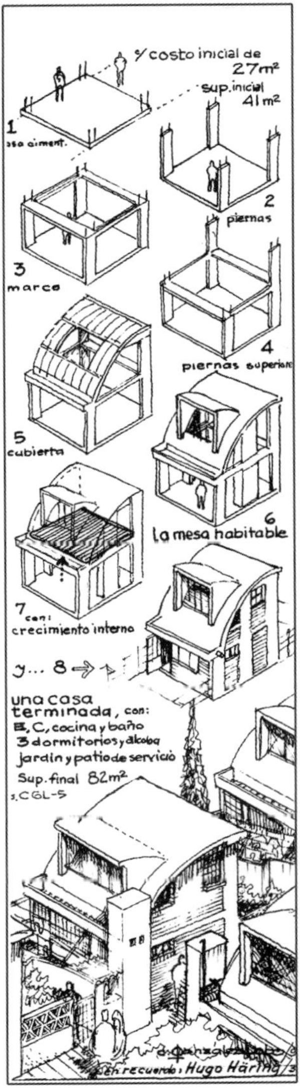

Carlos González Lobo. The table home.

staircase creates different spaces at mezzanine levels. The site plan shows houses distributed around a communal courtyard for a neighborhood community to develop.

Carlos González Lobo demonstrated that collective participation combined with an architect's technical support can produce high-quality living spaces for users to identify with their culture without being forced to live in anodyne boxes. With the right instruction, communities can self-produce their own habitats, innovating in both form and structure through reinforced double-curved vaults. Furthermore, these typologies' internal growth avoids any major, obvious transformations as happens in the following case study.

Carlos González Lobo. Shed House, Mexico.

Shed House. Axonometric drawing, side view.
Section and floor plans.

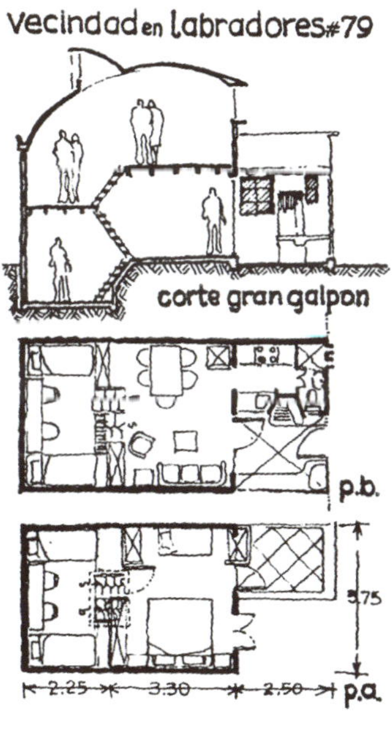
vecindad en labradores #79
corte gran galpon
p.b.
5.75
2.25
3.30
2.50
p.a.

HOUSING

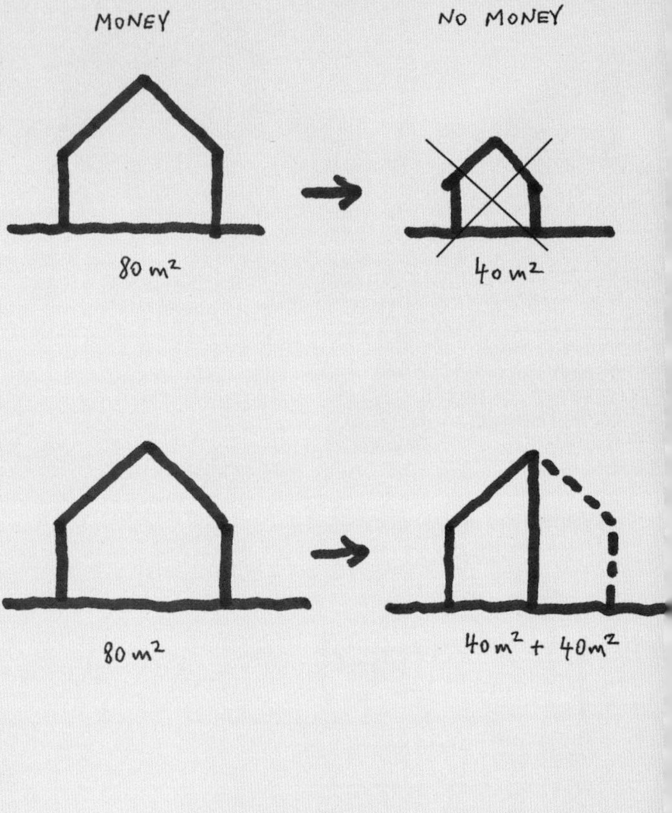

Diagram by ELEMENTAL showing that half of
a good house is better than one bad house.

ELEMENTAL

Various attempts have been made to understand the logic of self-built housing in order to integrate it into manufacturing processes, just as expert architects have worked with communities to rationalize participatory building. In the case of Mexico, Carlos González Lobo, like many other architects in Latin America, tried to rationalize spontaneous constructions, while Oscar Hagerman has worked alongside communities to design their houses and community centers. In both cases, the architects have been closely involved and therefore made a local impact.

Alejandro Aravena's Chilean studio, ELEMENTAL, poses the same questions: Can a house be truly flexible without incorporating future growth and self-built housing processes? In *Incremental Housing and Participatory Design Manual,*[12] the studio responded to the need to adapt housing over time. The analysis is based on some certainties in order to compensate

12 Aravena, Alejandro; Iacobelli, Andrés, *ELEMENTAL: Incremental Housing and Participatory Design Manual.* Hatje Cantz Verlag, Berlin, 2012.

for the government's inaction, assuming that any middle-class family can live reasonably well in a 70 or 80 square-meter home. But the studio asks: What if that isn't enough space? "Public policies and the market have developed two strategies to compensate for insufficient resources: building in more remote locations and on a smaller scale. When money is lacking, the tendency is to build on plots in peripheral areas where the cost of land is very low, and to construct 30 to 45 square-meter housing units."[13] And families respond to small spaces by building extensions however they can. Aravena concludes that half a good house is not the same as a small house, something that government policies fail to understand; in fact, it is most efficient to build the half of the house that a family on their own would be unable to do. They also realized that the sum of individual actions (even when competently executed) does not ensure overall quality or the common good. The idea of planning incremental housing is not new; it dates back to the 1960s. ELEMENTAL therefore asks: What is new? Being expandible does not mean leaving the construction half-finished in the hope that the individual owner might complete it. Expandability must be designed. Applying common sense and the principle of least effort, when designers of the initial form need to plan ahead for the second half that will enable each family to reach a middle-class housing standard. The home—they go on to say—is an investment almost by definition, although sadly this is not

13 Aravena, Alejandro; Iacobelli, Andrés, *ELEMENTAL*, p. 14.

ELEMENTAL. Quinta Monroy. Iquique, Chile, 2004.

the case with social housing. ELEMENTAL takes the view that "housing should be more of an investment than a social expense, an instrument to overcome poverty and not just provide shelter."[14] Therefore, instead of placing housing developments on low-cost land, the studio proposes giving them access to the network of opportunities found in cities, based on the principles that they should be sufficiently high density, low-rise (dispensing with hard-to-maintain collective spaces such as corridors and elevators), not overcrowded, and expandable (bringing middle-class living standards within reach over time).[15]

ELEMENTAL sees the need to redensify urban areas, in the understanding that the city has been a very efficient human invention to improve people's quality of life, particularly for the poorest sectors of society. For Alejandro Aravena "the city is practically a public health mechanism, a vehicle for survival."[16] Cities are basically a concentration of opportunities: for work, education, healthcare, mobility, and even recreation. However, ELEMENTAL also points out that "if governments and markets cannot react in time, people will not go to cities; urbanization will emerge from encampments" in a process that will sadly "increase the proportion of people excluded from the benefits and opportunities concentrated in

14 Ibid., pp. 17-18.

15 Ibid., p. 21.

16 Ibid., p. 24.

cities." The conclusion is that "generally speaking, we can produce housing when resources are plentiful. We can also produce low-cost housing of a poor quality. The challenge is knowing how to build houses that are both affordable and of a high quality."[17]

ELEMENTAL seeks to make growth possible, since buildings cannot accept individual extensions except (horizontally) on the ground floor and (vertically) on the top floor. ELEMENTAL's contribution has been to design a sufficiently porous house for it to be expandible within the structure itself, within the volume's outline. This idea creates a hybrid between a house (offering growth potential) and a building (for its high-density and efficient use of the available land). In turn, the studio emphasizes the importance of location, making it essential to have a sufficiently high density. This density must be achieved by giving each property direct and individual access to the ground floor, avoiding vertical circulations and shared horizontal corridors because these spaces spawn social conflict and urban deterioration. For Aravena, designs must provide sufficiently high densities in low-rise constructions, avoiding overcrowding and allowing for future growth. In this way, "self-built housing no longer needs to be seen as degenerative but as an alternative means of personalizing urban space."[18]

17 Ibid., pp. 26-28.

18 Ibid., pp. 37 and 490-493.

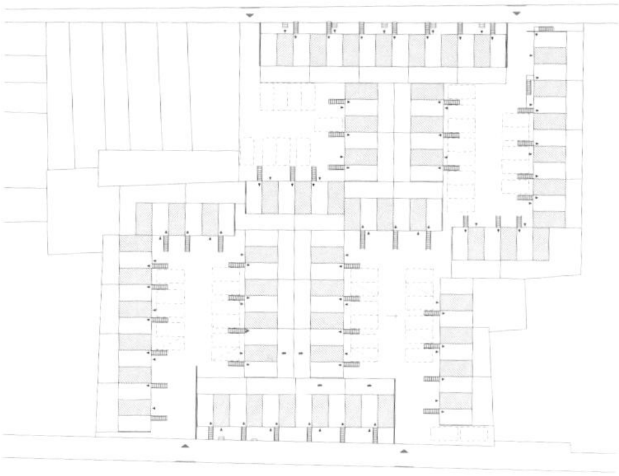

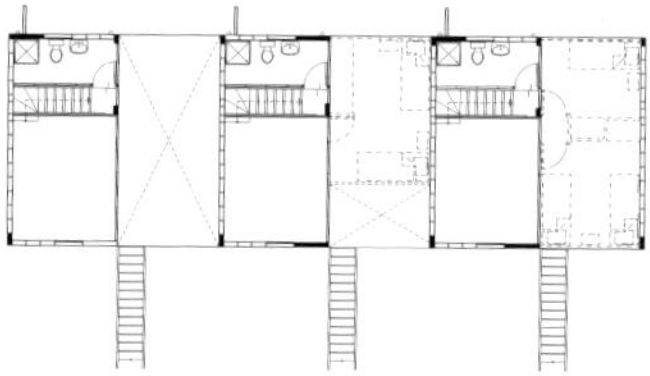

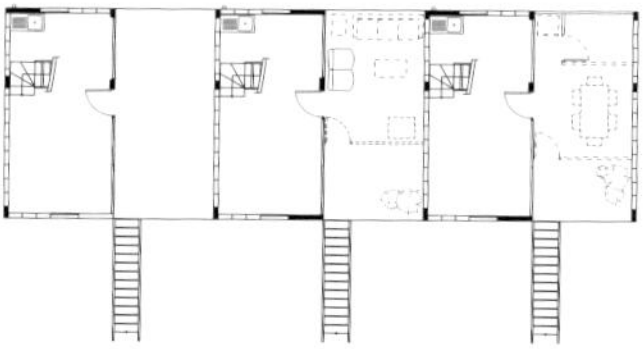

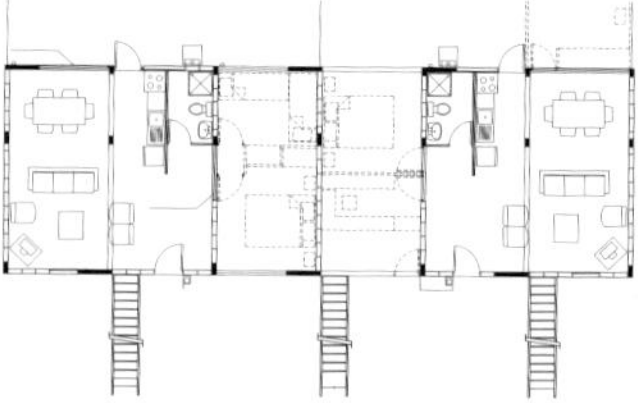

Quinta Monroy. Site and floor plans of ELEMENTAL's first progressive social housing project.

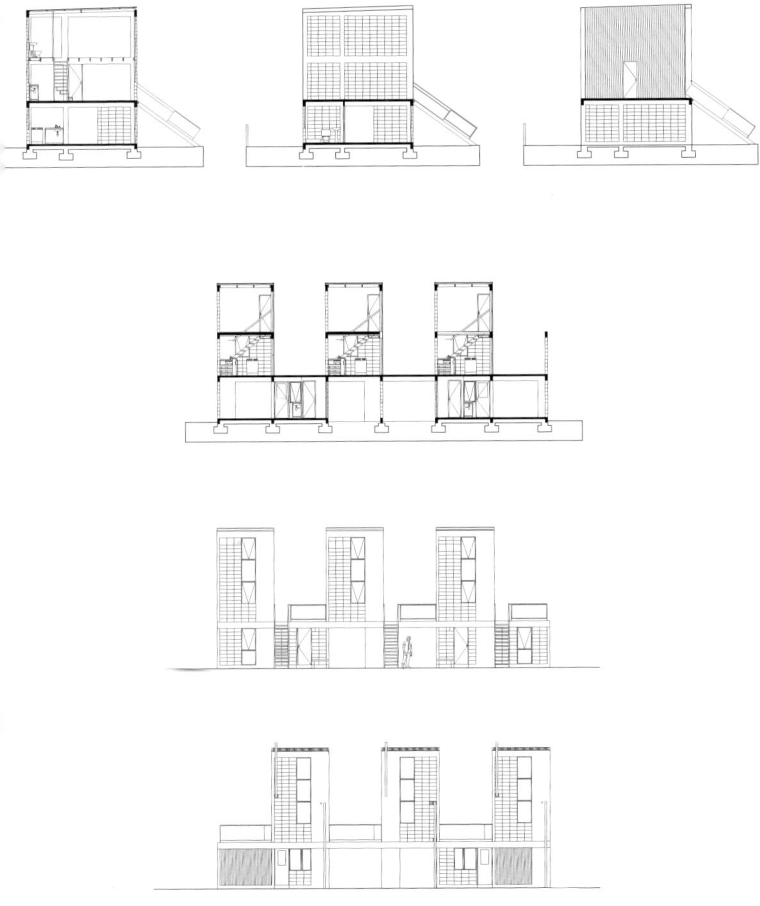

Sections and façades of the residential units.

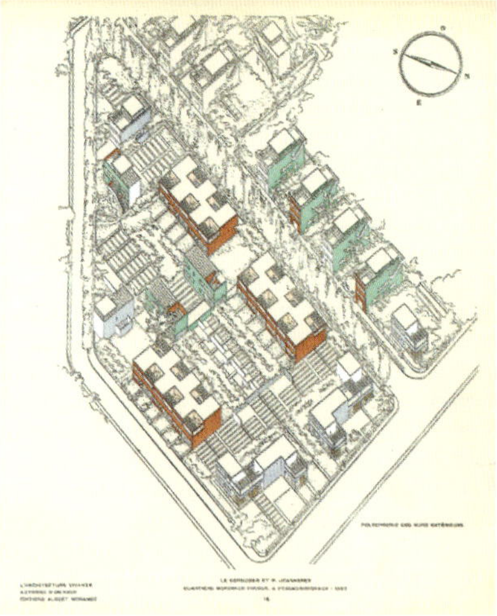

Despite ELEMENTAL's very innovative approach, a precursor exists of the same idea in Le Corbusier's Cité Frugès, Pessac, France (1926), where the Swiss architect explored the potential of expandible housing.

ELEMENTAL. Las Anacuas. Monterrey, Mexico, 2009.

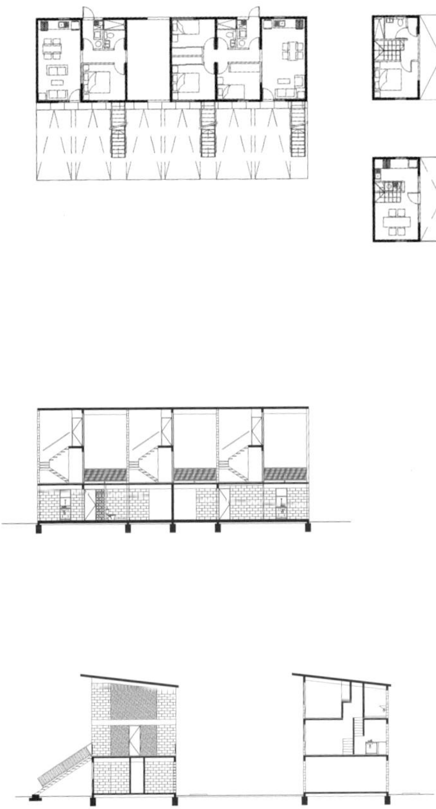

Floor plans and sections of residential units.

ELEMENTAL, Villa Verde, Constitución, Chile, 2014.

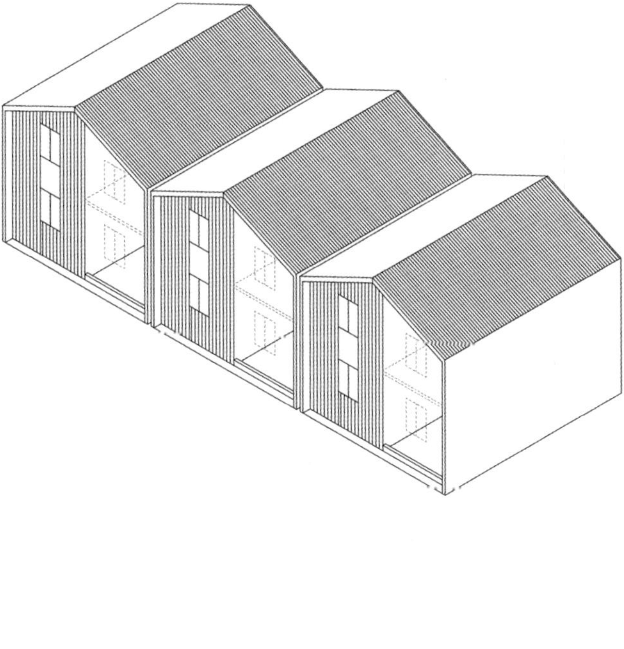

Axonometric view of residential units.

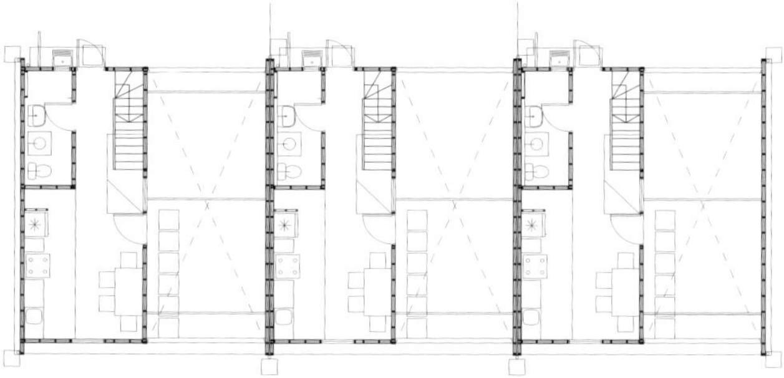

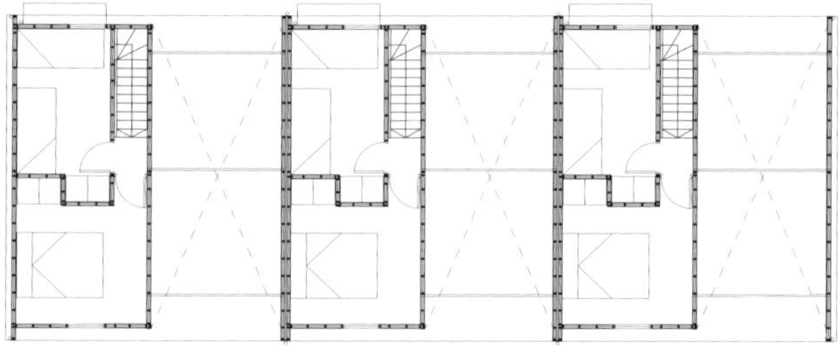

Floor plans of residential units.

ELEMENTAL. Villa Verde, Constitución, Chile, 2014. Before and after assisted self-built housing process.

Diagram by JC Arquitectura / Juan Carral showing the "smart density" housing concept.

Suburban redensification: recent Mexican case studies

In Mexico, after a period of some notable social housing proposals in the 1970s, an endless isomorphic scab of shrunken houses began to spread around the outskirts of every city, stimulated by Infonavit funds[19] that prioritized quantity over quality and sought the lowest-possible land cost—regardless of the expense of the infrastructure needed to connect these peripheral areas to cities. This led to abandoned homes and no added value.

A natural disaster was the straw that broke the camel's back. The September 2017 earthquakes razed more than two hundred thousand homes in Mexico and starkly revealed something that was already known: many people with few resources live in self-built homes or isolated state housing developments.

19 Infonavit is a tripartite institution in Mexico that includes the participation of state workers, the private sector, and the government. It is perhaps one of the world's largest financial institutions for social housing, approving 1,500 mortgages a day.

Instead of solving the housing problem, both these situations worsen it: self-built housing is precarious and government-built housing stock is unsustainable. Houses constructed by people themselves, without technical expertise in structures and installations, produce a minimum or insufficient habitat for most of the Mexican population. In many cases, homes have been informally appropriated, depriving occupants of rights of ownership or government support in case of collapse, as happened after the earthquakes. Social housing made available through Infonavit mortgages have also failed to deliver a solution.

In recent years, Infonavit's research center for sustainable development (CIDS, for its initials in Spanish) has generated a set of ideas and proposals replicable on a large scale and based on the idea that rampant growth has been a failure and that land is the most valuable and scarcest of urban resources, making it essential to manage it for the benefit of society. In turn, research and proposals developed over the past century are given due recognition, from case studies of the Modern movement's mass-produced housing to examples of residential blocks built in Latin America and Mexico, and most recently in Japan and Chile.

Following trials with three housing prototypes developed by Juan Carral O'Gorman in the state of Tabasco, as well as others in the Donceles neighborhood on the outskirts of Cancún, 32 projects

COLONIA DONCELES **2015**

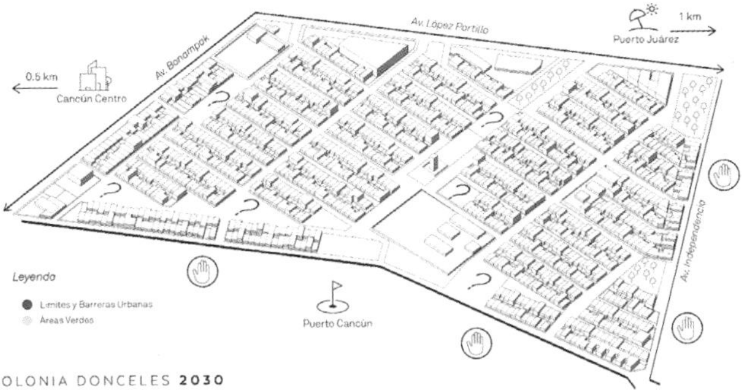

COLONIA DONCELES **2030**

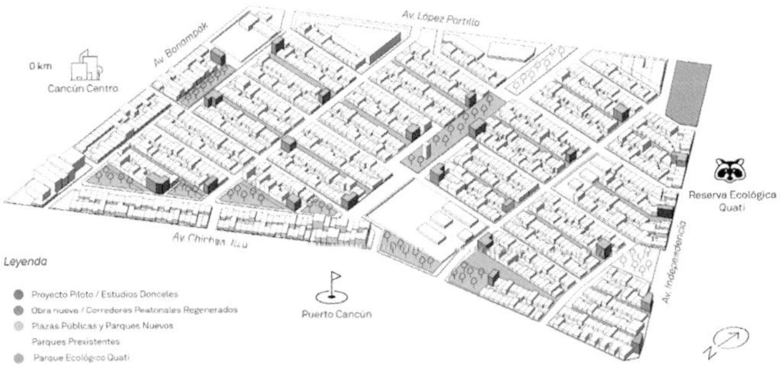

Strategic urban acupuncture projects designed by JC Arquitectura / Juan Carral in the low-income neighborhood of Donceles in Cancún, Mexico.

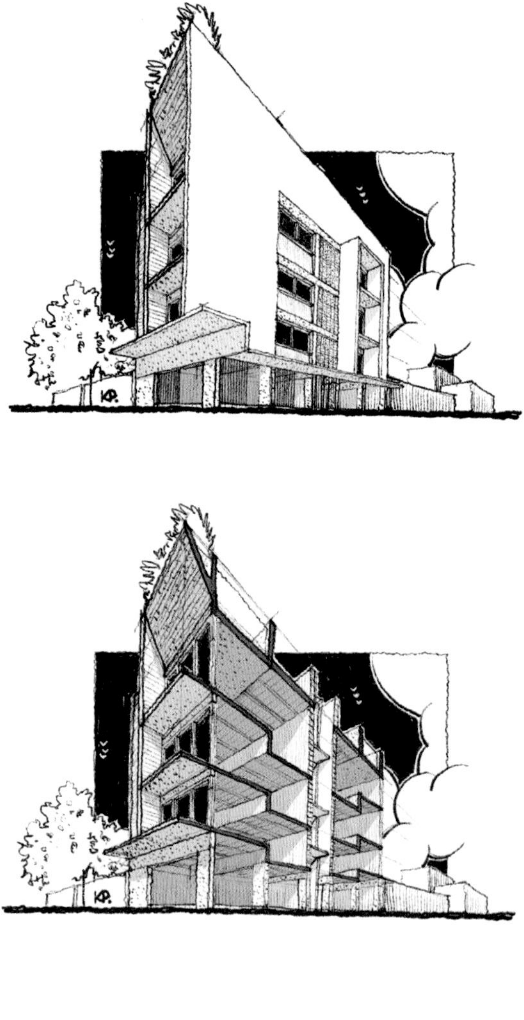

Donceles, section perspective.

replicated the same concepts in different suburban areas in 15 municipalities in 13 states across Mexico. These projects display a range of typologies that ensure social diversity and offer flexibility. Depending on each plot's surface area, the buildings consist of six flexible units (two per floor) measuring at least 38 square meters, as well as a ground-floor retail space and a green communal roof terrace. They also improve the urban surroundings. In terms of social housing, Juan Carral speaks of smart density in reference to "superstructures" of four or five stories consisting of a ground floor with some amenities or retail spaces, and three or four stories with different housing typologies.[20]

The CIDS proposals, led by Carlos Zedillo, "make recommendations to encourage more consolidated and compact land-use planning that implies combining time schedules, processes, and actors as a platform of management-action to improve people's quality of life." As Zedillo points out, "these projects have different typologies to guarantee social diversity; they are proposals that define new needs, new spaces without hierarchies and that, in the vast majority of cases, offer flexibility. These projects prioritize collective and transitional spaces through elements such as plazas, terraces, and balconies."[21]

20 *Redensificación Urbana*. Published by CIDS (Infonavit) and Arquine. Mexico City, 2018, p. 51.

21 Interview with Carlos Zedillo, May 15, 2020, Mexico City.

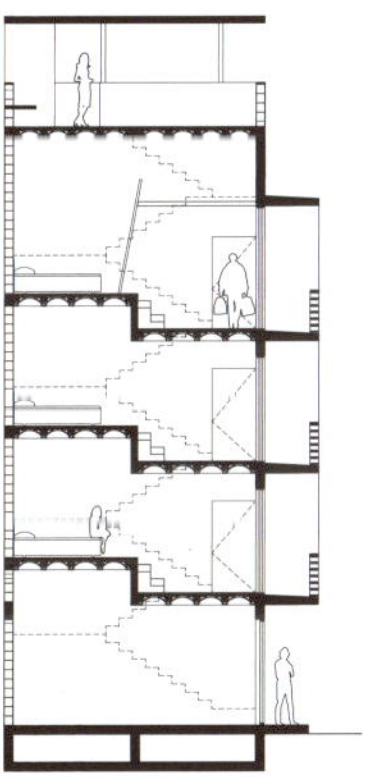

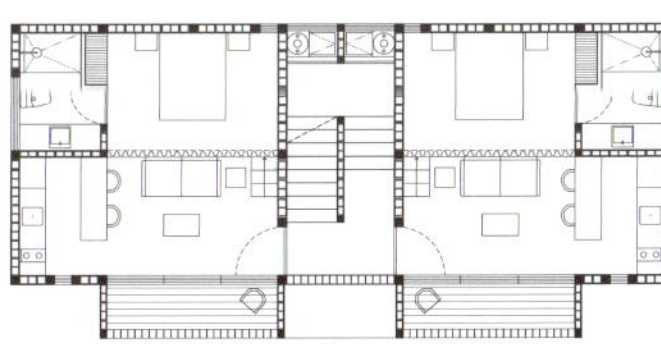

JC Arquitectura / Juan Carral, D7, 2018.

MIQUEL ADRIÀ

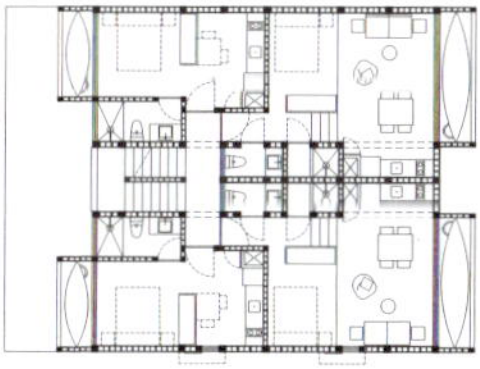

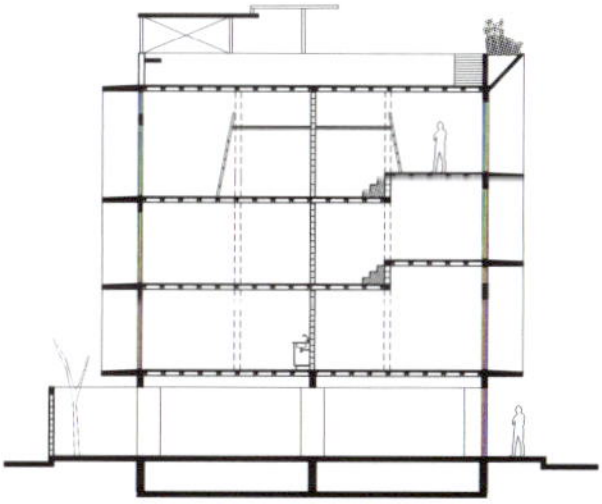

JC Arquitectura / Juan Carral, D10, 2018.

Urban redensification project. Models of different housing proposals.

Of the 32 projects, some notable examples have explored and contributed typological innovations, or understood the critical importance of typological and distributive efficiency in minimum dwellings. Among the former, DVCH's design stands out for concentrating its entire program of services around the perimeter of small, square-plan housing units. Bathrooms, kitchens, closets, and alcoves on the perimeter free up ample, open spaces for multiple uses in the center. PRODUCTORA and other studios focus on efficiency, with central staircases and two apartments per story, and in their case with particularly successful results. Jorge Ambrosi and Gabriela Etchegaray create a stripped-down typology that they had already developed based on a central ribbon containing all the building's services and stairs, adding special complexity to these small apartments. Alberto Kalach also builds on his own experiences—Sombrerete, Hermosillo, etc.—in a well-conceived approach which maximizes ceiling heights for minimum dwellings to increase their volume, and adds central mezzanine spaces or *tapancos* over the service areas.

Alberto Kalach's similar projects in Hermosillo confirm that the range of ideas and typologies from a century ago remain applicable for contemporary social housing. In this case, Kalach argues that a 70-square-meter house is not only better but also no more expensive than the 45-square-meter units being built by Sonora's social housing developers. Unlike these detached "boxes" with their

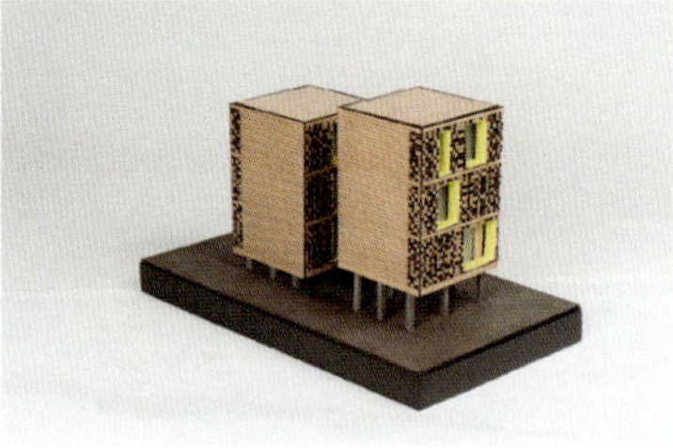

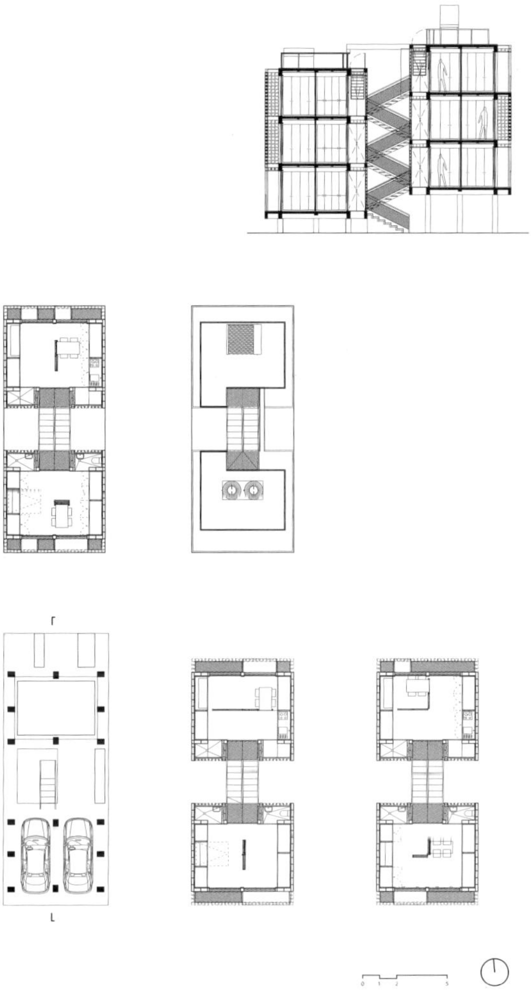

DVCH Devillarchacon Arquitectos. Valles del Sol subdivision. Culiacán, Mexico.

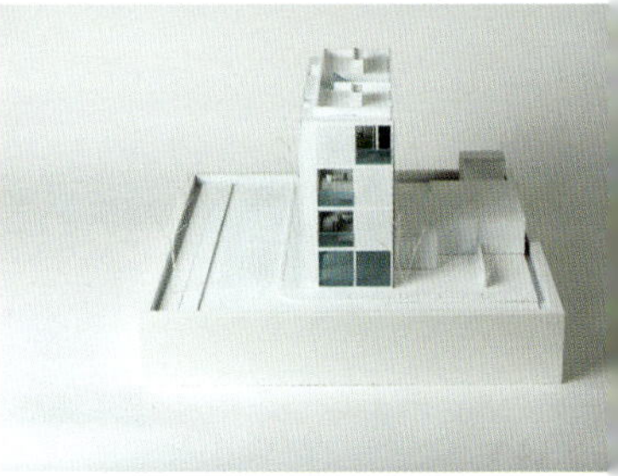

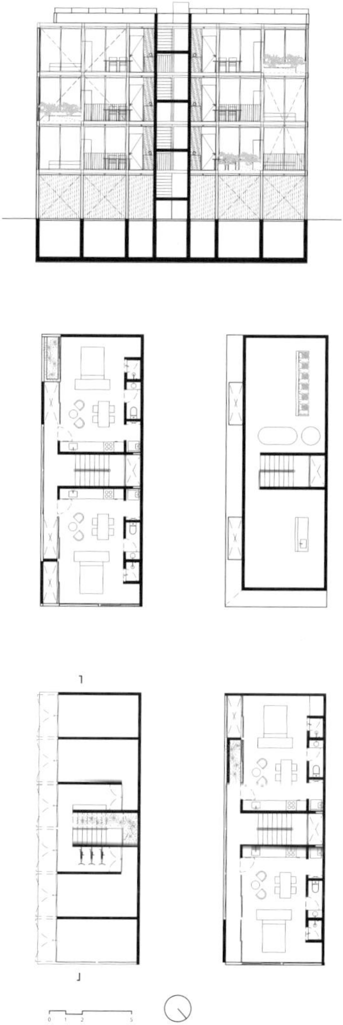

PRODUCTORA. Prados del Sur subdivision. Culiacán, Mexico.

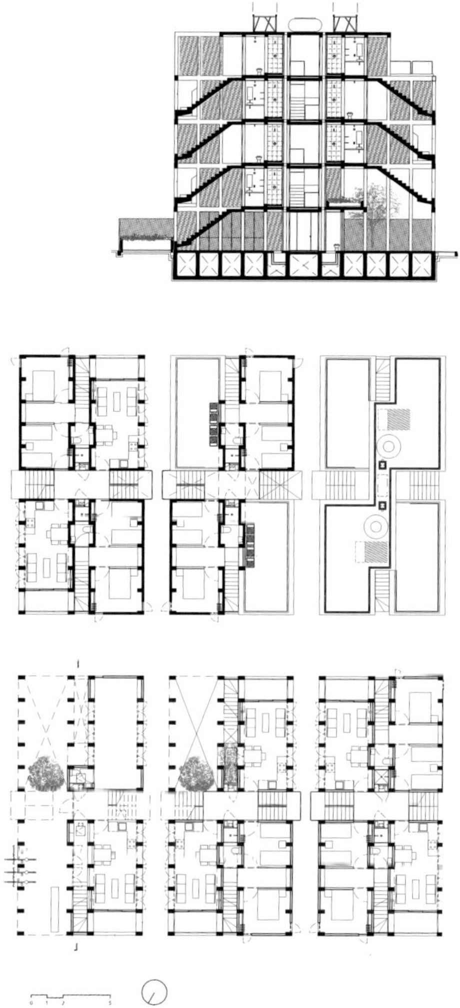

Ambrosi | Etchegaray. Lindavista subdivision. Tepic, Mexico.

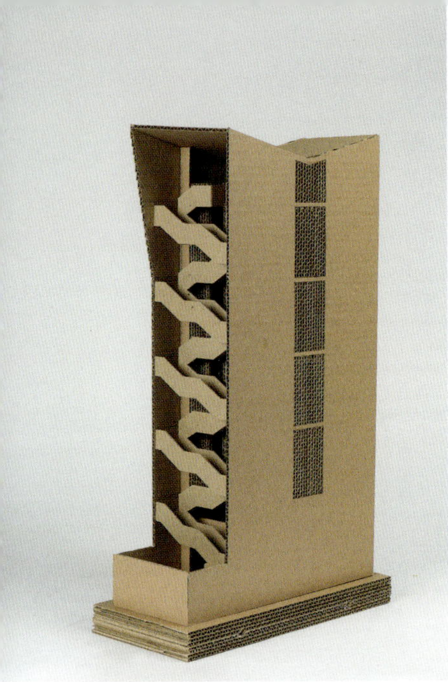

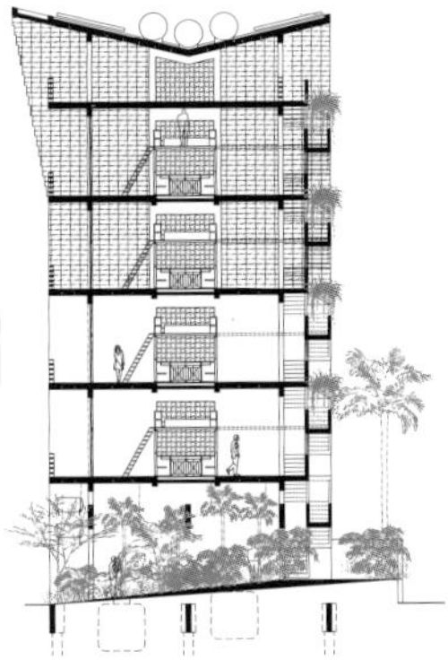

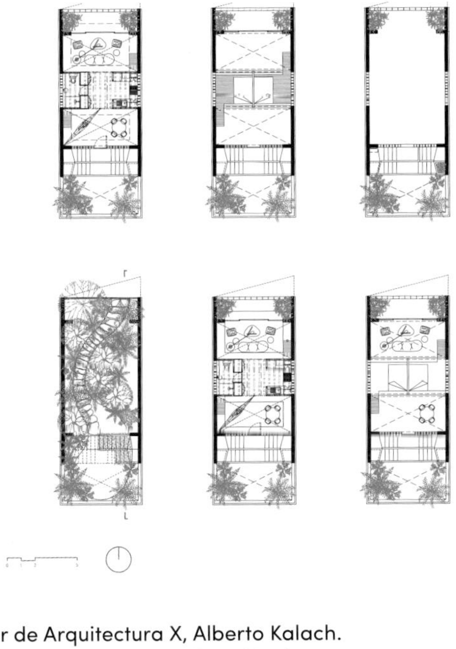

TAX | Taller de Arquitectura X, Alberto Kalach.
Súper Manzana 64. Quintana Roo, Mexico.

four façades, Kalach designs terraced housing (with only two façades and party walls) as well as a section with mezzanine levels that create more spacious units.

Such examples can be replicated as a first step toward offering real estate market typologies that improve upon obsolete social housing models. Positive examples can persuade developers and local governments that such small constructions encourage urban redensification on the outskirts of towns and add value.

Based on this research, Carlos Zedillo concluded that "what is becoming clearer than ever is the need to consider housing models that bring together private and public spaces using intermediate spheres, and that make a positive impact on the structure of the urban context. In this sense, the *Urban Redensification* project sought to make the city, one housing project at a time."[22]

22 Interview with Carlos Zedillo.

TAX, Alberto Kalach. Sketches of Bosco Residencial. Hermosillo, Mexico, 2019.

TAX, Alberto Kalach. Bosco Residencial.
Hermosillo, Mexico, 2019.

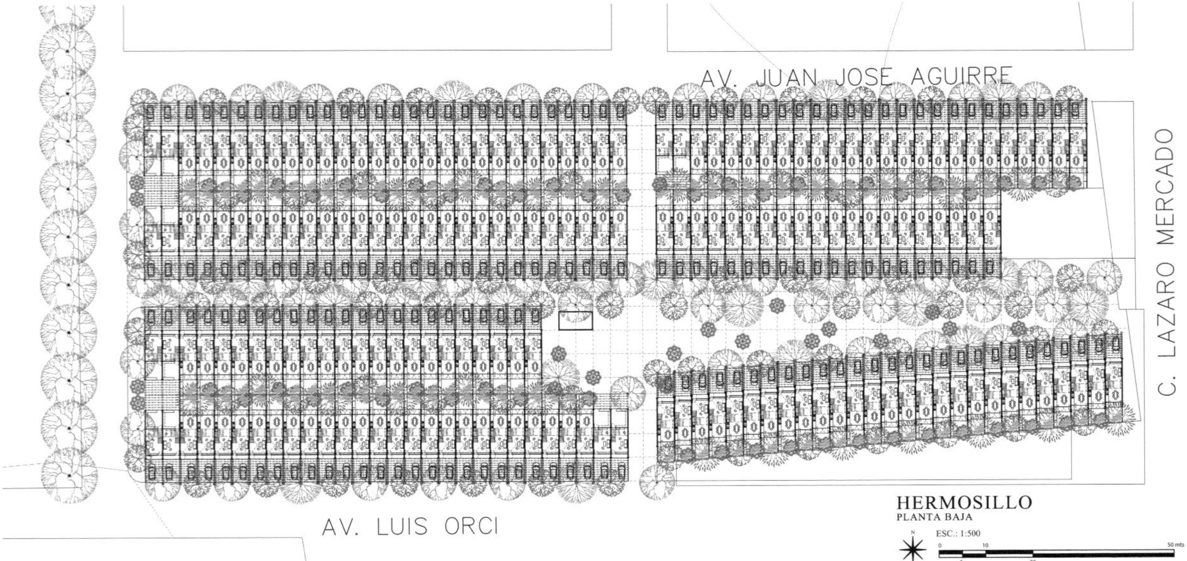

HERMOSILLO
PLANTA BAJA

VEGETACIÓN CONJUNTO

MEZQUITE CHILENO HIBRIDO	21 piezas
AFRICANO - AFRICAN SUMAC	46 piezas
ACACIA SALIGNA	48 piezas
WASHINGTONIA ROBUSTA	11 piezas

VEGETACIÓN PATIOS

PALO VERDE "DESERT MUSEUM"	26 piezas
ACACIA SALIGNA	25 piezas
WASHINGTONIA ROBUSTA	51 piezas

CASAS	180
TERRENO	16,618 m2
LOTE TIPO	68 m2 (18.68m x 3.66m)
M2 CONSTRUCCIÓN POR CASA	63.5 m2
M2 COMERCIO	115 m2
M2 PLAZA	2,158 m2

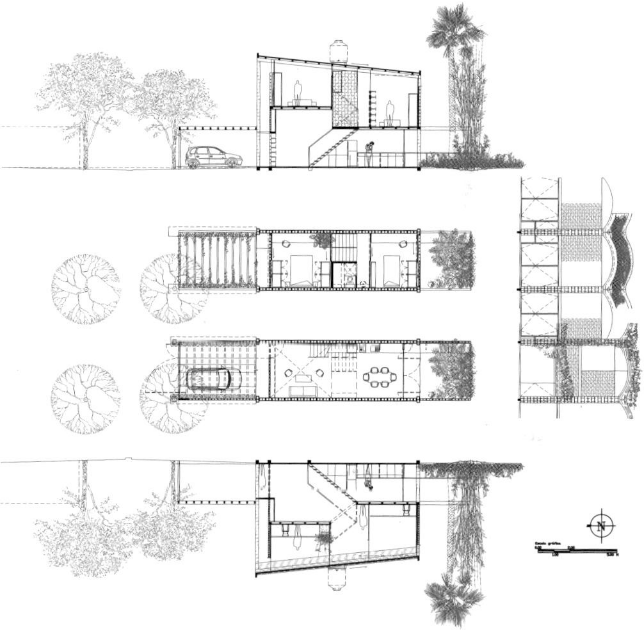

Bosco Residencial. Site plan, sections, and floor plans.

Manuel Gausa, Actar Arquitectura. Barcelona Forum. Barcelona, Spain, 2004.

Typological transformation and flexibility

In the 1920s and 30s, researchers defined the principles of social housing then being developed around the world based on stereotypical nuclear families. But by the end of the 20th century, these evolved toward greater typological, distributive, and functional diversity, in a process that continues to this day. In this sense, dimensional and ergonomic studies on minimum dwelling, as well as planning manuals (Neufert, etc.) have helped in the design of domestic spaces. However, we have largely inherited a bourgeois housing model that has been compressed to varying degrees, based on a series of specific functions for each space: a dining room for eating, a lounge for a living space, a kitchen for cooking, a bedroom for sleeping, and a bathroom for washing. This was not always the case and some good exceptions exist: Rudolph Schindler's house-study in Los Angeles, where four diaphanous living spaces were joined two by two with a shared bathroom, freeing up courtyards and gardens, as well as a bedroom for working in and transforming food (a kitchen, you might call it) for the four rooms. Some other very particular cases also provide exceptions to the systematic repetition of the same program, with one, two, or three bedrooms for certain family stereotypes. However, the nuclear family of father, mother, boy, and girl certainly no longer exists as an archetype but only as one among an almost infinite variety of potential configurations of users. This diversity has prompted new research and ideas. Manuel Gausa identified that housing, and social housing in particular, continues to be highly conventional,[23] and he drew up research based on a new programmatic definition. Housing as an archetype has evolved due to changes in lifestyles. The transformation of the family unit (childless couples, roommates, etc.) as understood and analyzed for middle-income sectors does not take into account social housing, which still repeats the same model developed 70 years ago. We need to recall that "fluctuating labor markets and eventually moving house requires units that appreciate in value and that the coparticipation of active members in the family economy implies less time spent on fewer domestic chores, creating a new concept in server spaces,"[24] hence Gausa proposes the need to redefine the inhabited space through multi-use spaces.[25] By appealing more to diversity than to repetition or mixed sections that enable various (horizontal

23 Manuel Gausa, *La vivienda: nuevas alternativas y sistemas*, Actar, Barcelona, 2002, p. 15.

24 Ibid., p. 19.

25 Ibid., p. 21.

Manuel Gausa, Actar Arquitectura. Barcelona Forum.
Barcelona, Spain, 2004.

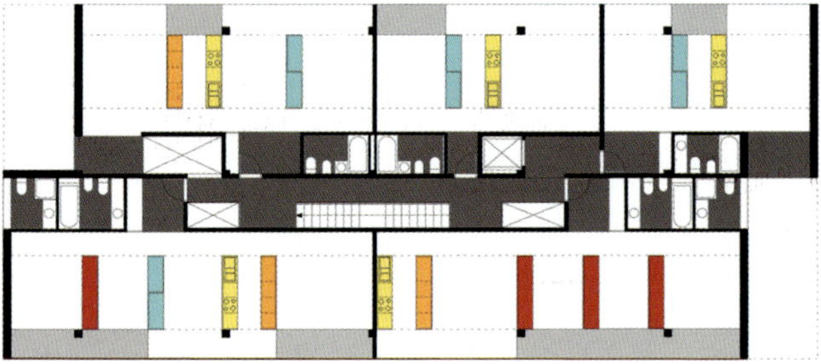

Barcelona Forum. Initial layout based on functional strips and floor plans of final design.

and vertical) solutions, dynamic typologies appear in response to the exploration of the limits inherent within contemporary projects and their ability to generate new formal devices.[26] Ideas that react to open systems as opposed to closed compositions, eventually, as Mark Wigley points out, develop a prosthetic vocation,[27] ranging from thick walls that concentrate all services to free up the maximum available space (for eating, sleeping, working, playing, etc.), to movable partitions that can alter the spatial layout throughout the day and at night, maximizing each housing unit's flexibility and potential. Whereas ELEMENTAL proposes doubling the space assigned to social housing through expandability, Gausa compensates the spatial limitations with prefabricated systems and walls containing services, placing more faith in the industrialization of architectural elements and in recycling than in self-built or artisanal housing.

Following Gausa's ideas published in *Housing: New Alternatives, New Systems* implemented by the author in several of his own projects, many ingenious ideas surfaced that turned time into an important factor in transforming domestic spaces. Prime examples of the benefits of flexibility and typological transformation include Andrés Jaque's minimum

26 Ibid., p. 23.

27 Wigley, Mark, "Prosthetic Theory: The Disciplining of Architecture." *Assemblage* 15, 1992 and *Ottagono* 96, 1992, p. 11.

SISTEMA "ABC"

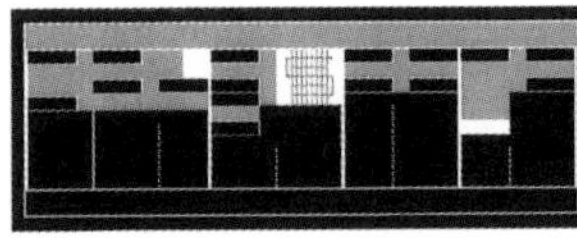

SISTEMA "FULL-BACK"

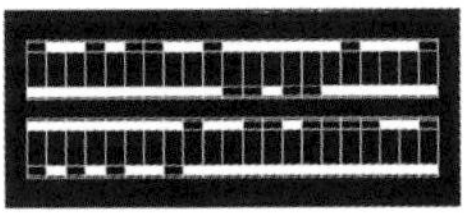

SISTEMA "RAIL"

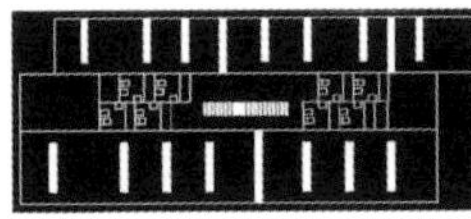

SISTEMA "BARE-CODE"

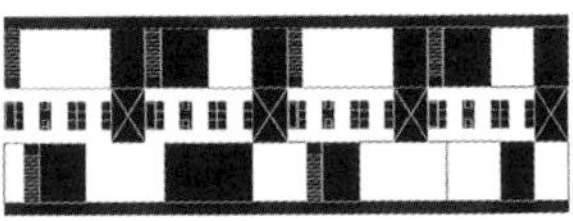

SISTEMA "1 - 0"

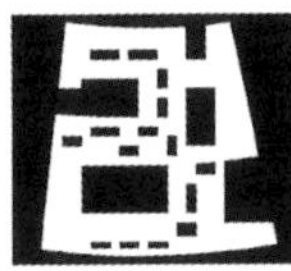

SISTEMA "ELEMMENTAL"

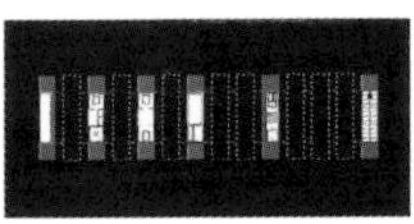

SISTEMA "M'HOUSE"

SISTEMA "WALL'HOUSE"

Gausa + Raveau, Actar Arquitectura. Diagram of combinatorial models. Variable evolution/development systems, 1990–2010.

dwellings that incorporate mezzanine levels (*tapancos*) and transform the rigidity of housing in open-air parks and domestic gardens, or the apartments transformed into stackable bookshelves by ENORME Studio (Carmelo Rodríguez and Rocío Pina).

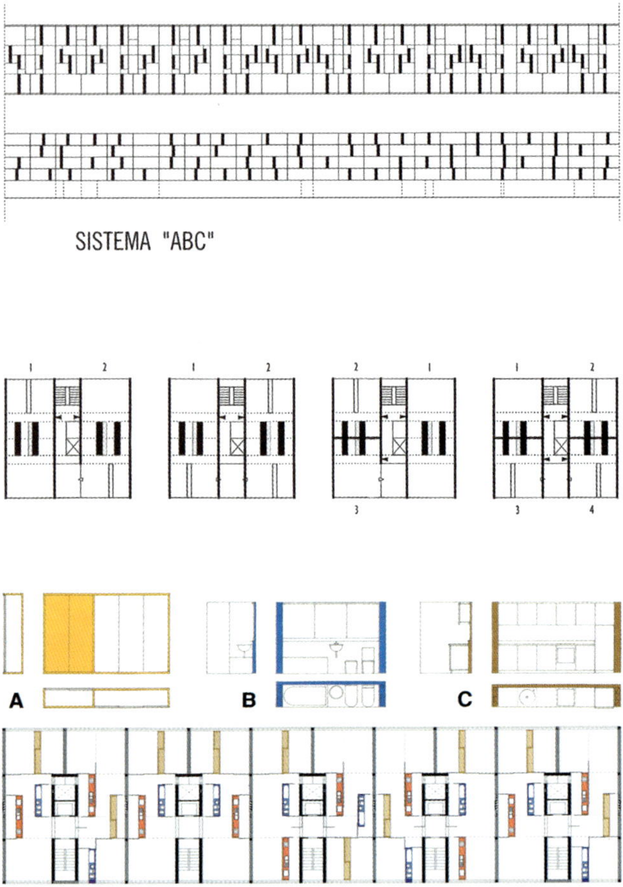

ABC System. Variable distribution matrix referred to semi-prefabricated equipped modules. Built area: 35 m^2–70 m^2

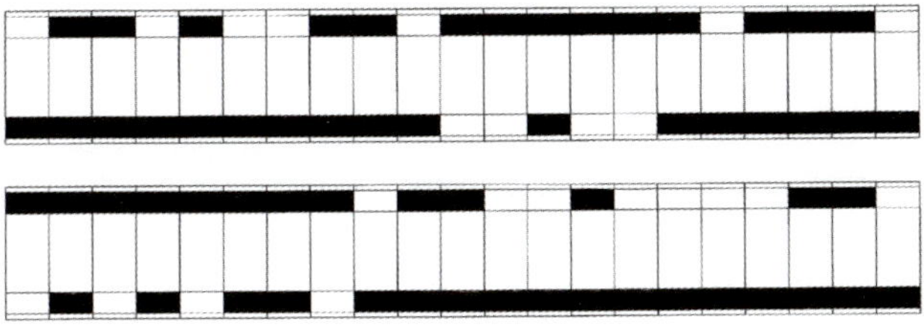

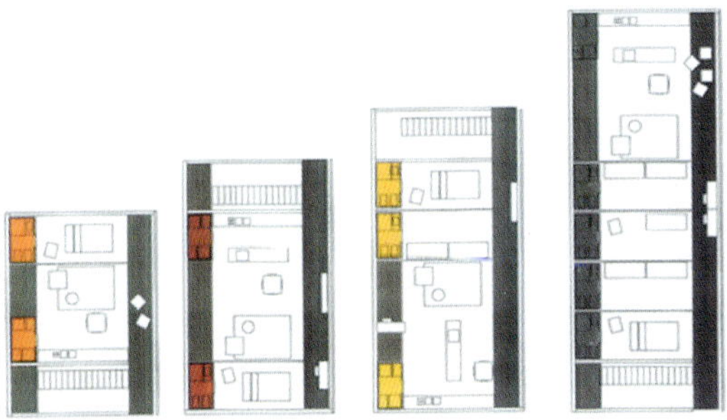

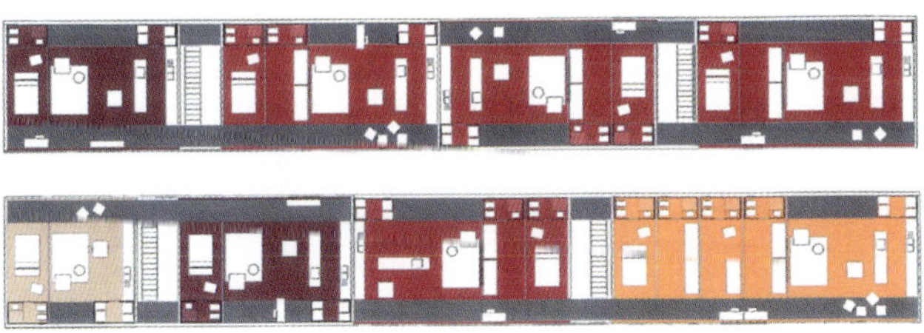

RAIL System. Development of residences with façade containing services and central living room. Built area: 40–90 m^2.

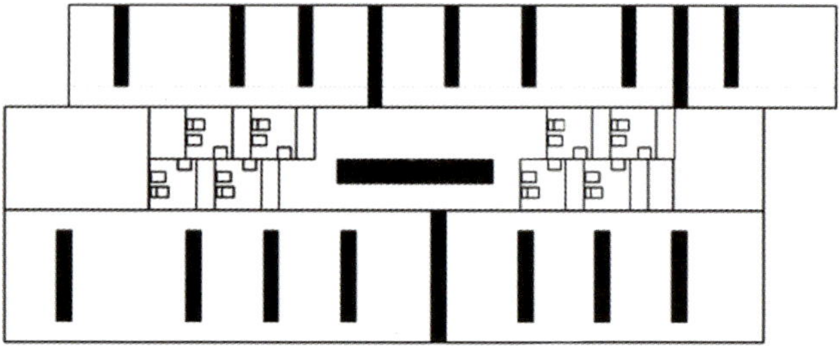

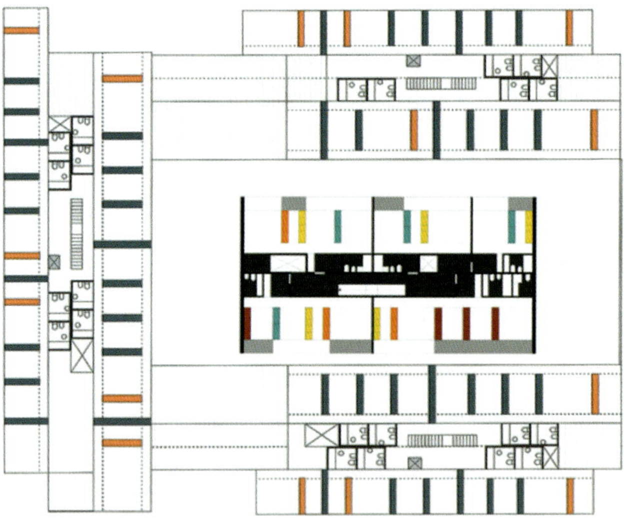

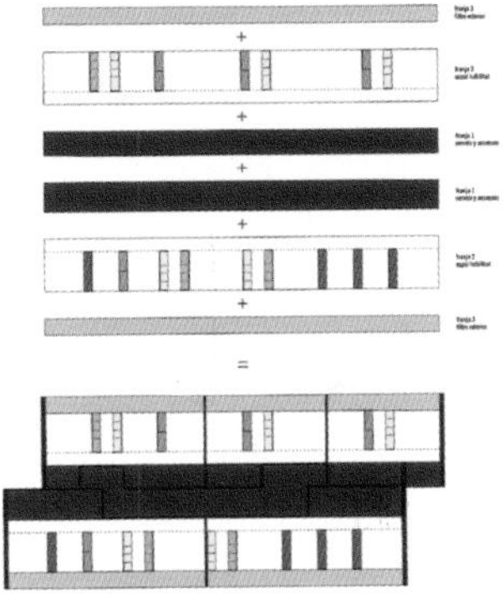

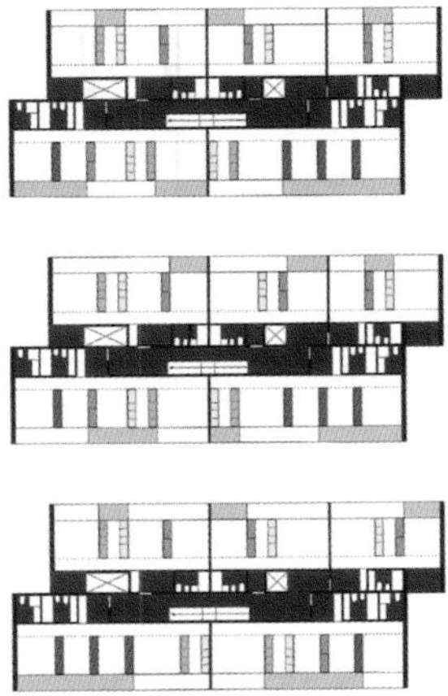

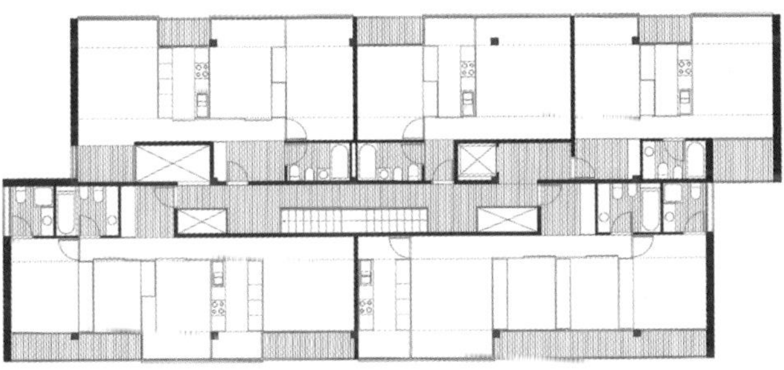

BARCODE System. Distribution with equipped nuclei connected to the central area and prepared lateral spaces. Built area: 50–90 m^2.

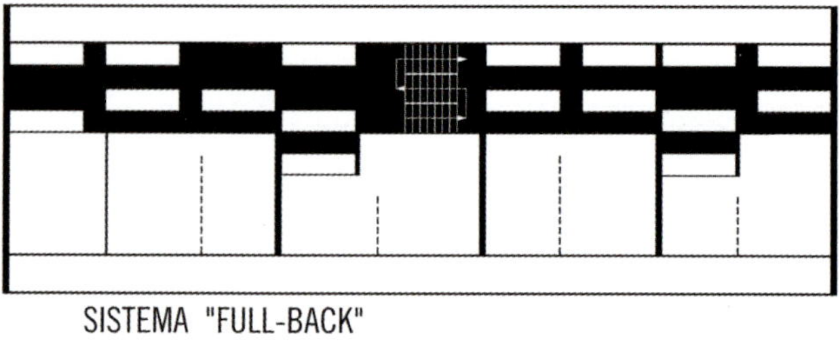

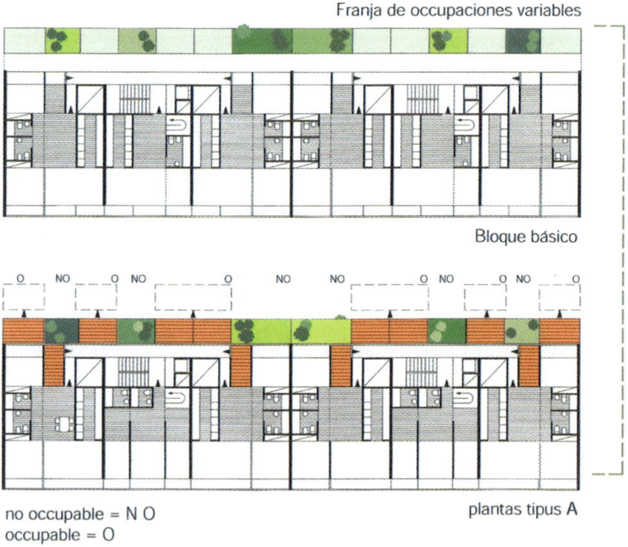

FULL-BACK System. Concentration of services at rear and frontal spaces with optimal views and orientation. Built area: 30–70 m^2.

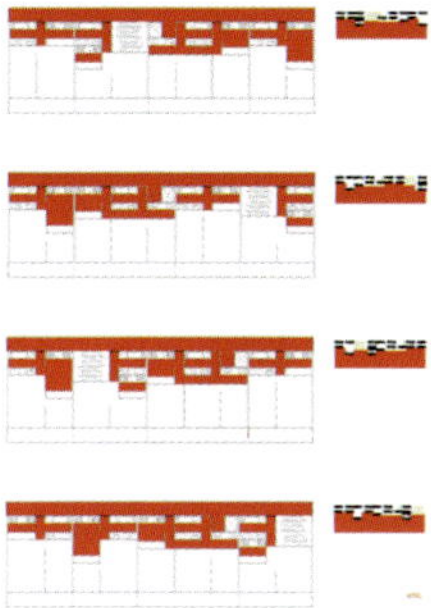

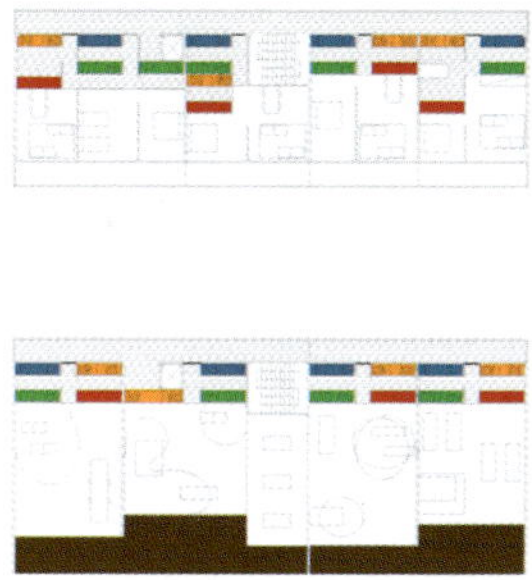

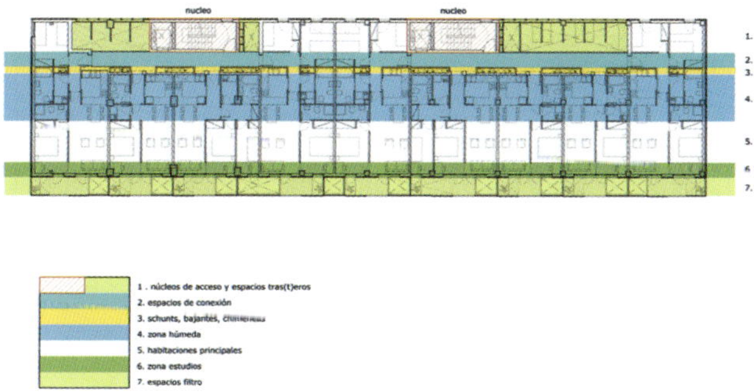
nucleo
nucleo
1.
2.
3.
4.
5.
6.
7.
1 . núcleos de acceso y espacios tras(t)eros
2. espacios de conexión
3. schunts, bajantes,
4. zona húmeda
5. habitaciones principales
6. zona estudios
7. espacios filtro

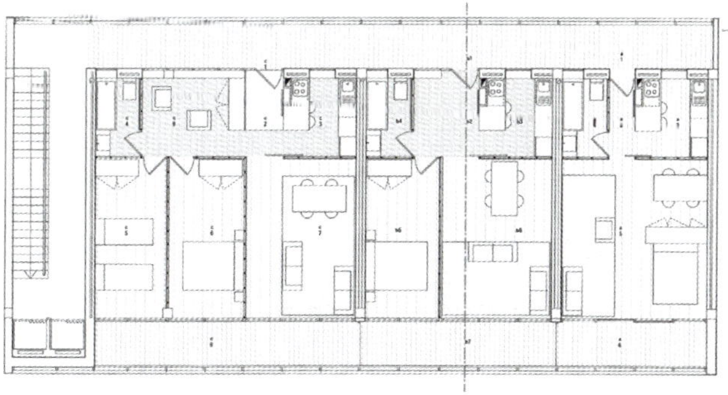

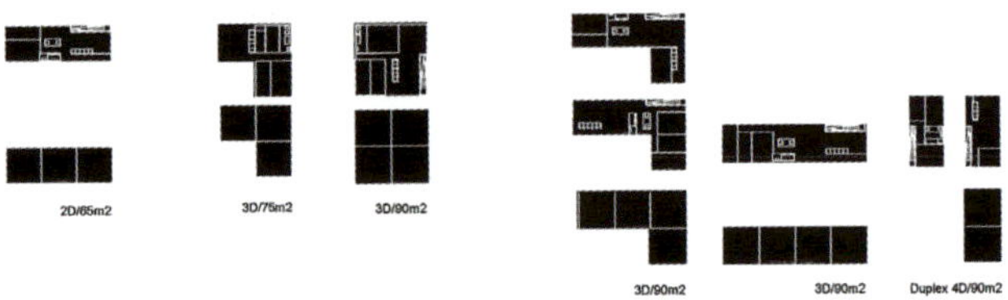

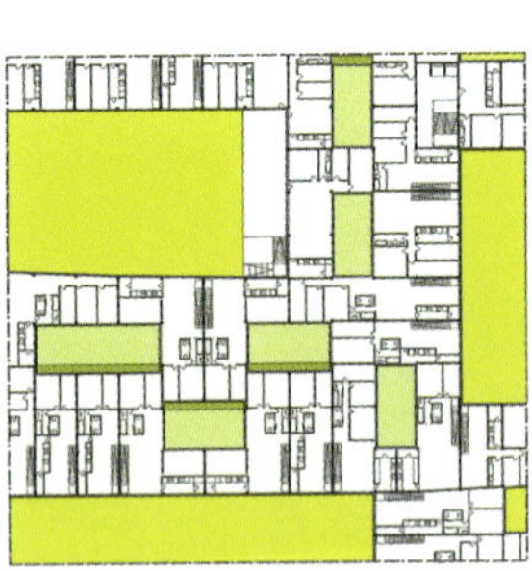

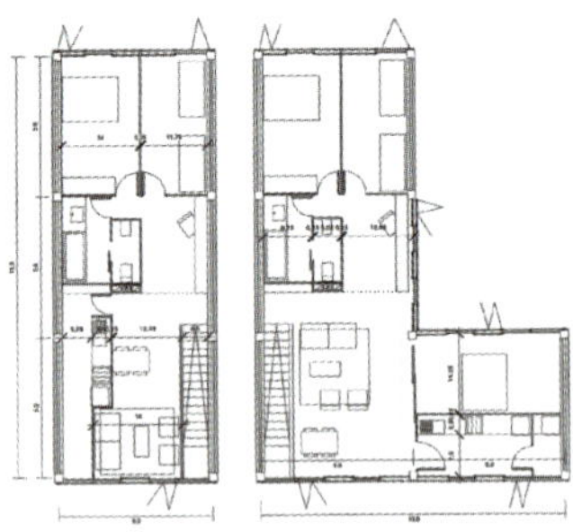

ELE(M)MENTAL System. Residential units with dual orientation in an alternating system of voids and courtyards with variable sizes and scales. Built area: 50–90 m^2.

planta baja patios | escala gráfica

planta segunda cubierta

planta cuarta cubierta

planta cubiertas total

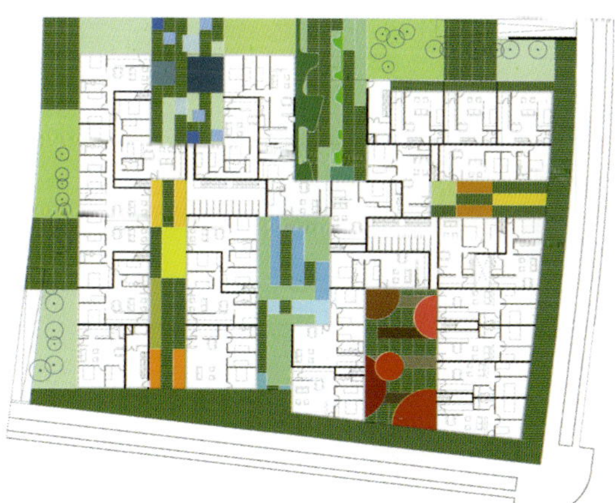

PKMN Architecture (now ENORME Studio). AIO House (All I Own House). Madrid, Spain, 2014.

ENORME Studio. EIP House (Everything in Place House). Madrid, Spain, 2017.

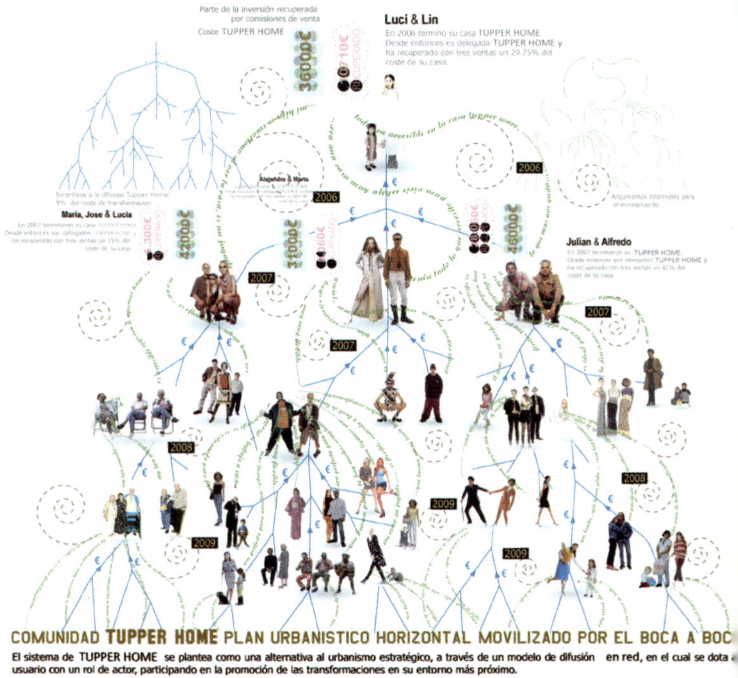

MIQUEL ADRIÀ

Andrés Jaque | Office for Political Innovation. Diagram of Tupper Home Society: Grassroots urbanism gaining scale through word of mouth.

Illustration from Yeung Hok Tak's *Qu'elle était bleue ma vallée.*

The Unité d'Habitation revisited: SANAA, OMA, and BIG

SANAA, OMA, and BIG are acronyms with much in common. The studios—led by Kazuyo Sejima, Rem Koolhaas, and Bjarke Ingels, respectively—demonstrate a shared belief in a model based on design strategies and diagrams to convert every project into a manifesto. Like Le Corbusier, in each case they build a narrative of the before, the during, and the after, in order to support their argument for the virtues of the original concept, the logic underlying the typology and construction, as well as the end result and both its local and global impact. In a discourse where everything fits neatly together, their ideas might seem obvious given the evidence of what came before them.[28]

Three of their housing complexes are heirs to Corbusier's Unité d'Habitation (UH) and break with typological paradigms: SANAA's apartment building in Gifu, Japan; OMA's The Interlace in Singapore, in collaboration with Ole Scheeren; and Bjarke

28 Adrià, Miquel, "Una vuelta de tuerca a la Unité d'Habitation," *Arquine* No. 75. Mexico City, 2016.

Ingels Group's VIA 57 West in Manhattan. One takes to the extreme the minimum living areas as per the UH model, another creates a vertical neighborhood with horizontal blocks, and the third blends two antonyms (a skyscraper and a block with a central courtyard). In each case, the floor-plan geometry is designed to achieve iconic impact.

Sejima's social housing complex is a single, very narrow block that zig-zags like the Corbusian redent; 10 stories contain 107 tiny apartments, which are the sum of various inhabitable prisms added horizontally and/or vertically. "Although the Gifu housing units do not conform to given typologies, they are all fully integrated into the rest of the building, which assumes complexity and reveals it in its sections, of interconnected housing units."[29] The circulation is limited to stairs attached to the façade structure, spanning the building's entire length. All of the bedrooms or cubicles face the side that receives the most sunlight and are joined by narrow, glazed terraces that function as intermediate spaces between interior and exterior. The rooms can therefore be closed, while the living areas extend outward to their respective glazed terraces.

The Interlace consists of 31 horizontal apartment blocks, each with six stories, stacked according to a

29 González Llavona, Adelaida, *Gifu-Kazuyo Sejima: El juego como método de proyecto y crítica de arquitectura*. PhD thesis at the ETSAM's Department of Architectural Projects.

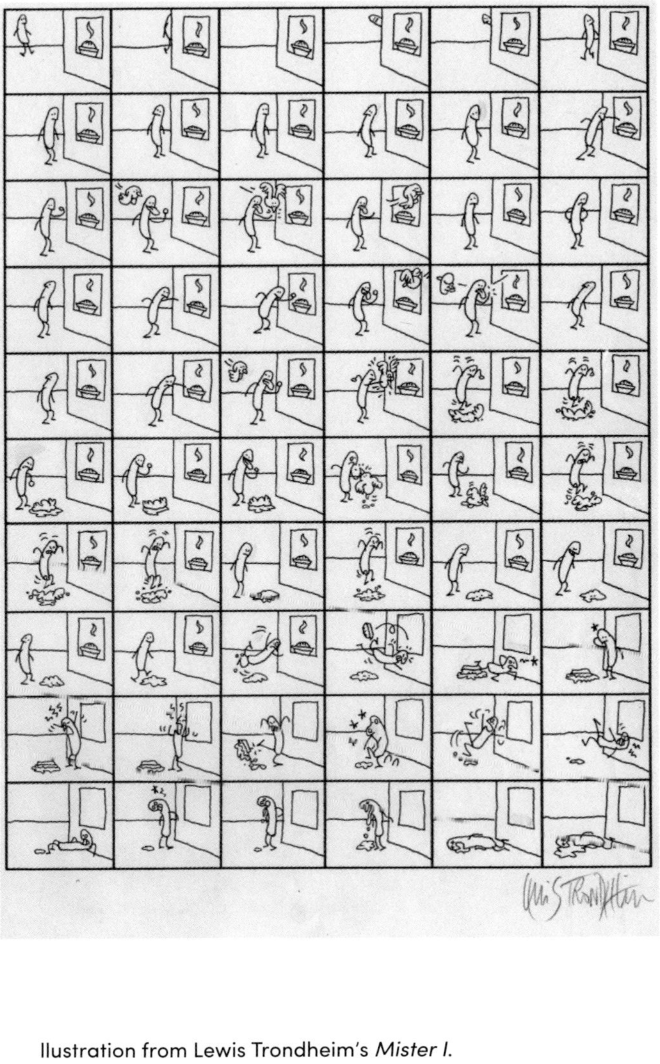

Illustration from Lewis Trondheim's *Mister I.*

Kazuyo Sejima & Associates. Gifu Kitagata apartment building. Motosu, Japan, 2000.

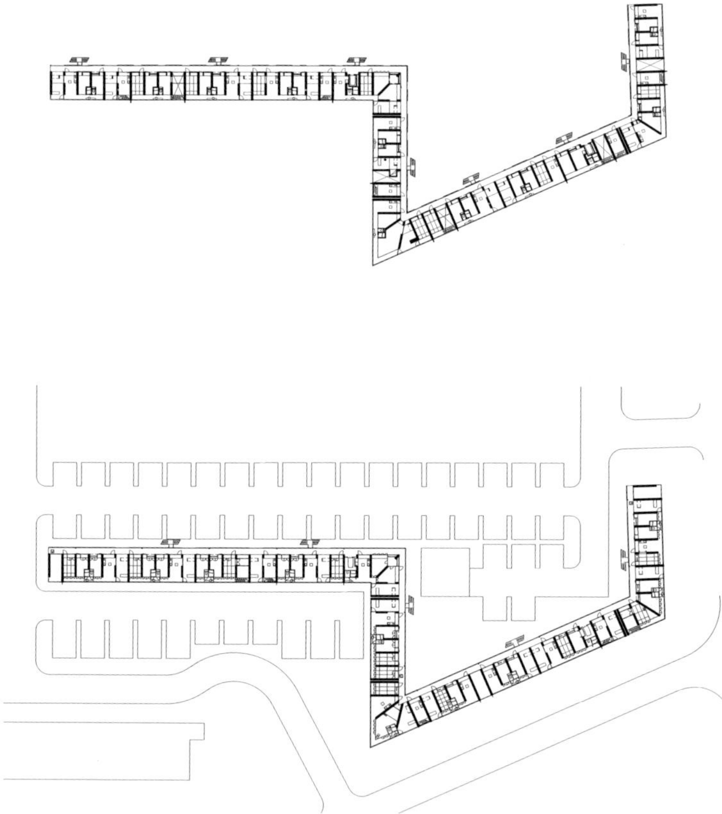

Gifu Kitagata apartment building.
Typical plan and ground-floor plan.

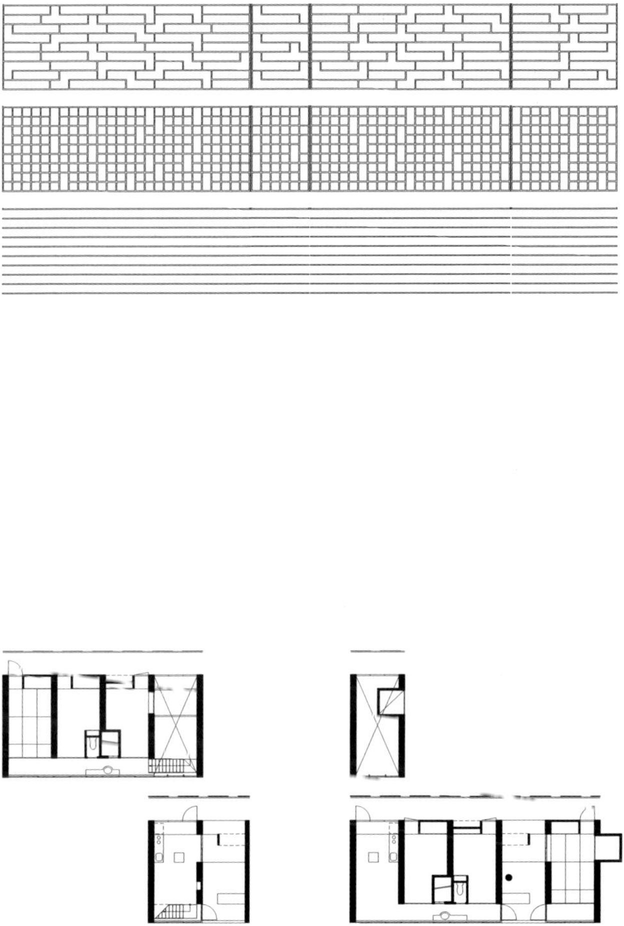

Sections and apartments typical plans.

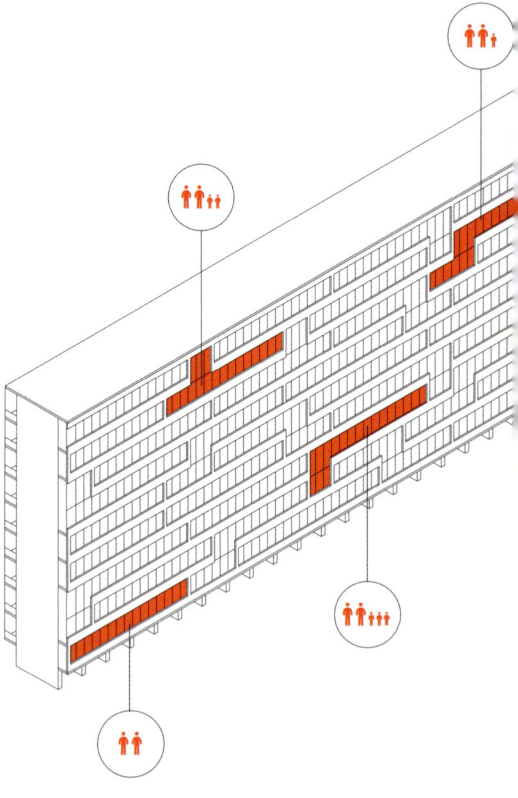

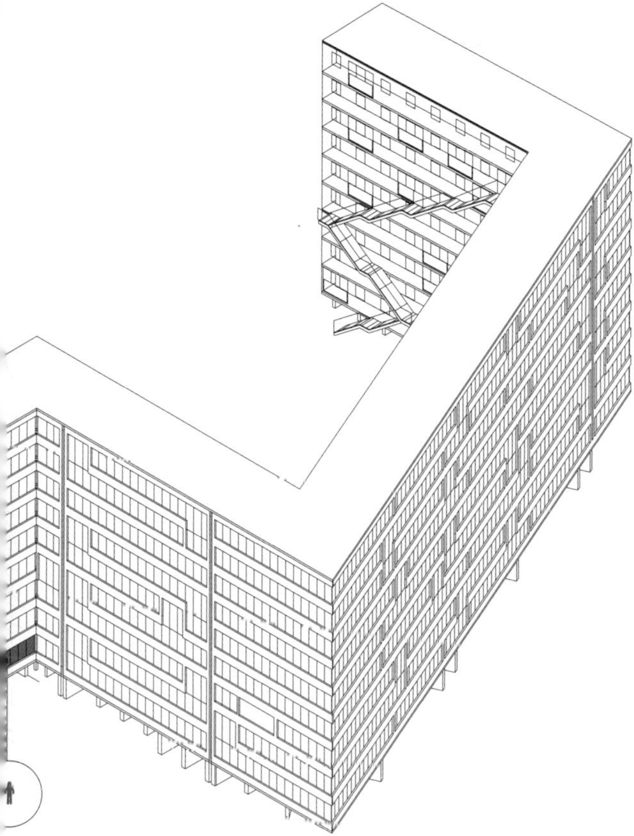

Axonometric view showing the residential units and number of intended occupants.

rigorous hexagonal plan that organizes the blocks on each side and creates eight large garden spaces. The blocks measure 70×22×16 meters and each one contains 30 apartments. They are piled up, one on top of the other, like in the game Jenga.

One of Singapore's largest and most ambitious residential developments, The Interlace boasts 170,000 square meters of built floor area, and 1,040 residential units on an eight-hectare plot beside one of the busiest urban highways of this tropical city-state. The apartments range in size from 75-square-meter two-bedroom units to penthouses with almost 600 square meters. Unlike the usual solution that would consist of 10 or 12 towers leaving leftover space in-between, the OMA/Ole Scheeren solution frees up large hexagonal spaces between the stacked horizontal blocks. Each one of the 31 residential blocks is anodyne, apparently simple yet requiring a sophisticated structure of bridges, since they are solely supported at each end. The blocks' juxtaposition creates a vertical neighborhood that reaches 24 stories in each stack of four, with open, shared, and private spaces on different levels, encouraging social interaction among neighbors. Tropical landscaping forms the heart of the complex and each apartment overlooks lush vegetation. The Interlace is a bold and intelligent alternative as an intricate residential complex with communal areas in a natural environment, as opposed to a zone of isolated skyscrapers devoid of any public space between them. That said, the much-vaunted

OMA / Ole Scheeren. The Interlace. Singapore, 2013.

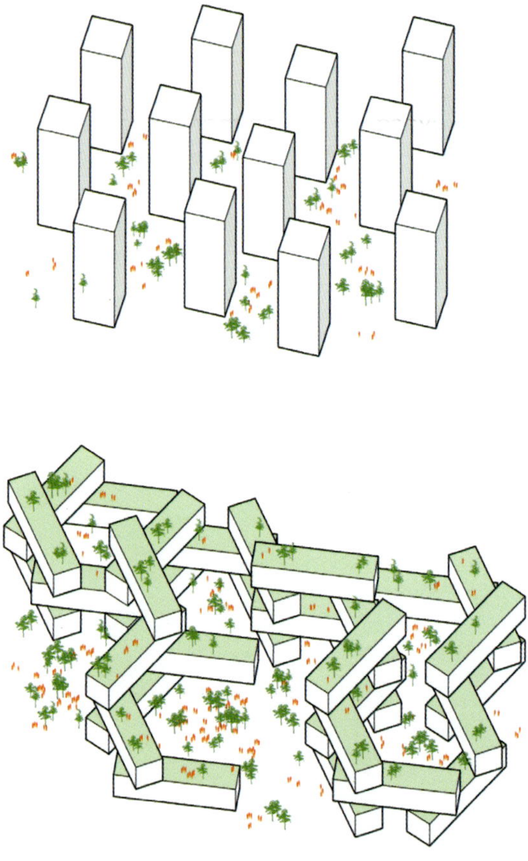

The Interlace. Conceptual diagram.

public space remains a private domain off-limits to non-residents, turning it into a hostile presence within the local area. Nevertheless, the project still makes an iconic impact with Koolhaas's characteristically provocative design that lies somewhere on the line between schematic and late-modern, combining the ideas of anonymous European postwar modernity with the cinematographic forms of future metropoli, blending residential units with the megastructures of 1960s utopias.

BIG's first project in the United States is located on 57th Street, beside the Hudson River in midtown Manhattan, between a power generation plant, a parking lot, and an urban highway. The 80,000 square meters of built space contains 709 apartments and a large central courtyard, as well as some 4,000 square meters of retail space. Residents also have access to a swimming pool, gym, basketball court, golf simulator, library, and movie screening room, as well as communal living areas, kitchens, and terraces. This residential complex is a "courtscraper," a hybrid between the New York tower on a base and a European block with courtyard, rising 142 meters high at its north-east tip. This design solution creates extreme asymmetry and a hyperbolic paraboloid surface with a pyramid shape affording views onto the Hudson River. Halfway between a roof and a facade, the resulting sloping stainless steel plane is perforated with south-facing terraces, creating views and maintaining privacy in each apartment. From the lobby, a large stairway

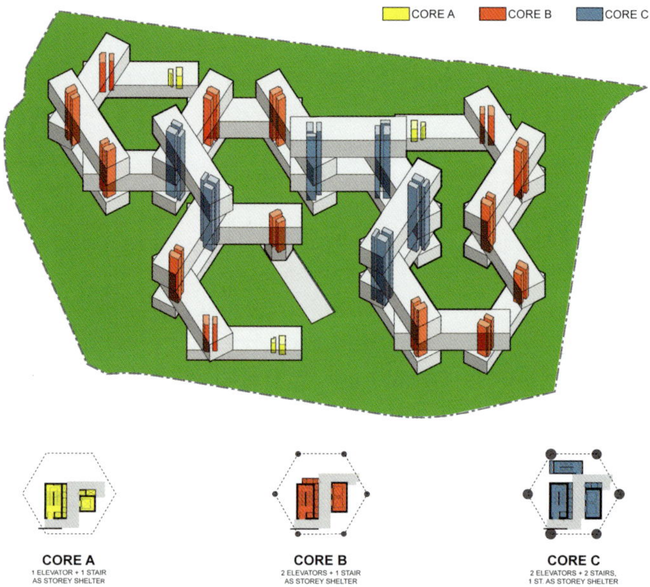

The Interlace. Circulation diagram.

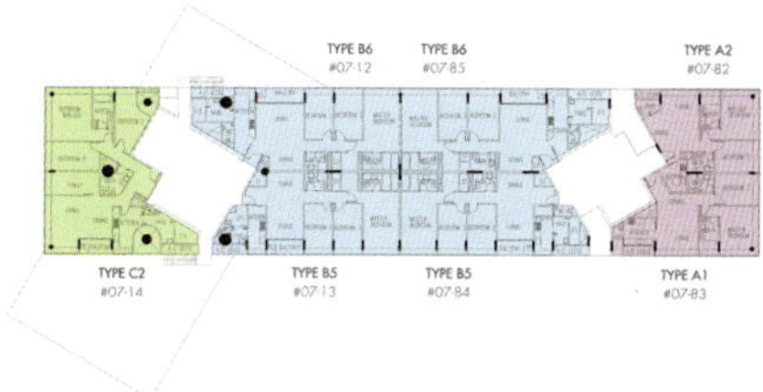

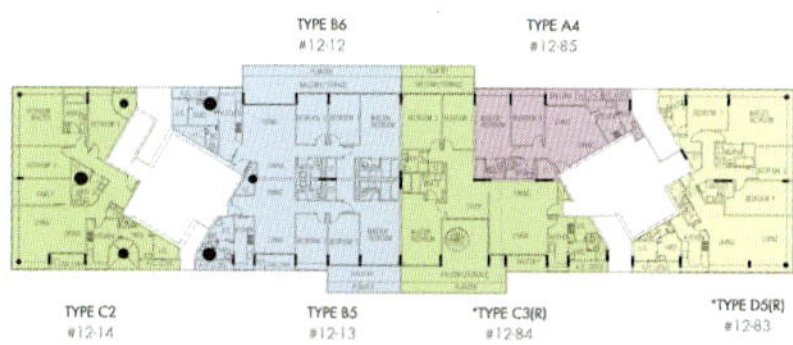

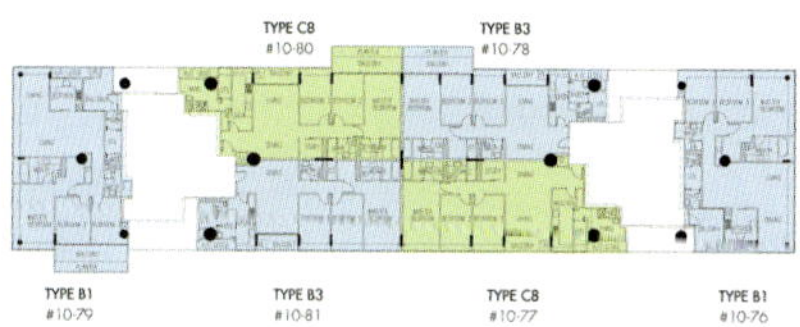

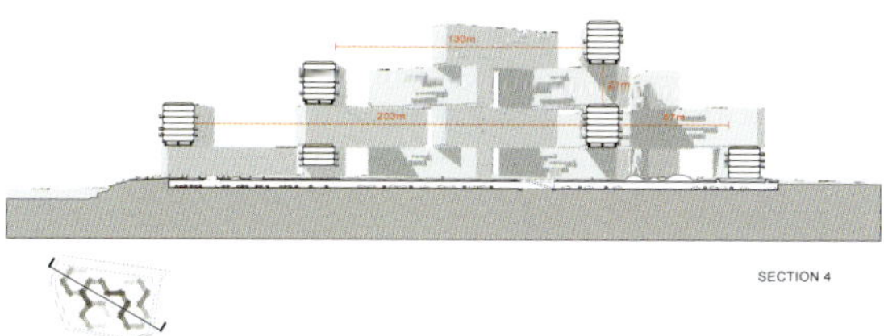

Floor plans and section.

leads up to the central second-floor courtyard, which has the same seasonal flora and the same proportion, albeit on a smaller scale, as in Central Park designed by Olmsted in the 19th century. This central courtyard displays the quintessence of European urbanism in the same way that Central Park is a metropolitan oasis and the heart of the city on an urban scale.

The massive artificial mountain—which has various forerunners in Copenhagen—is the accumulation of various typologies: the premodern skyscraper, the modern monolith, and the postmodern object. To some extent it returns to the mid-20th-century typologies that expanded the private program toward the exterior and integrated the public program within large complexes—a hybrid solution that combines the advantages of the perimeter block with a central courtyard and the skyscraper: European compactness and efficiency blended with the lightness and slender profile of the American skyscraper.

For Bjarke Ingels, architecture needs to be constructed in the same way as a child designs with Minecraft and should be buildable with Lego blocks. The project exists in the diagram and by adding what is essentially simple and incompatible: the courtyard and the skyscraper. And along the way, it also adds to Manhattan's iconic skyline.

These three projects are born of Le Corbusier's theory of the Radiant City, as autonomous high-rise

BIG | Bjarke Ingels Group. Via 75 West.
New York, United States, 2016.

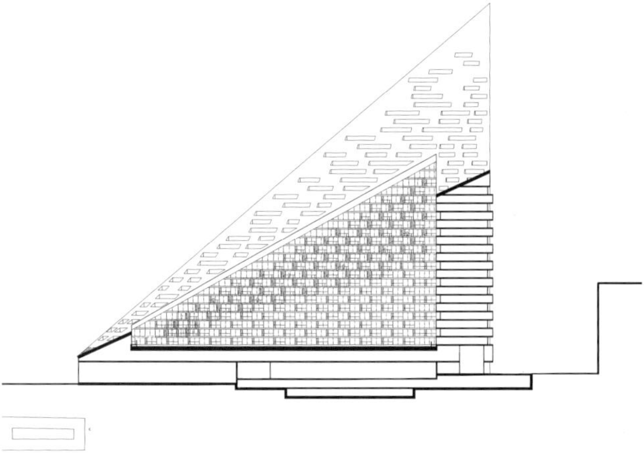

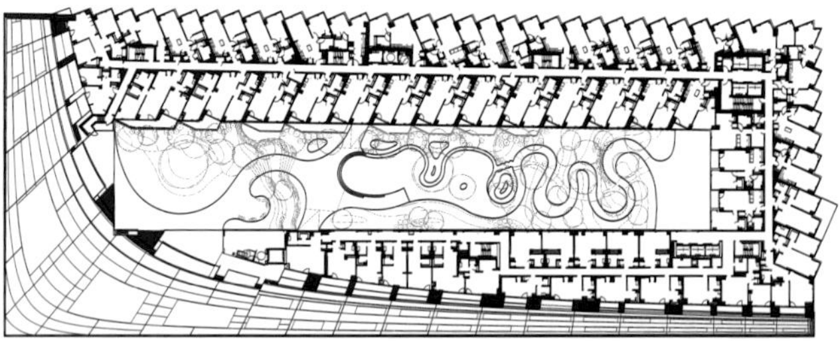

Via 75 West. Longitudinal section and level 4 floor plan.

buildings that create shared spaces with their required services. And they are largely fresh takes on the model of the Unité d'Habitation—adding Jenga, Minecraft, or Lego—as evolved around the world by the Candilis, Smithsons, and Panis over the course of the past century.

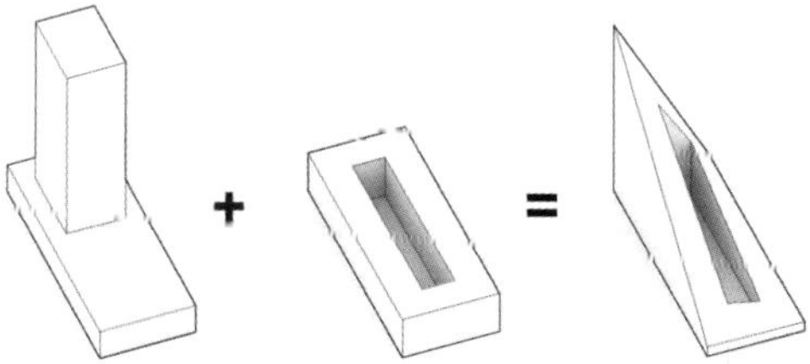

Conceptual diagram.

"Vacant NL" installation in the Dutch pavilion at the 2010 Venice Architecture Biennale, curated by Ole Bouman.

Recycling

At the 2010 Venice Architecture Biennale, Ole Bouman, curator of the Dutch pavilion, presented a catalogue, using models on the same scale, of all the buildings that have remained empty since the 17th century in Holland. The idea was to show the potential for occupying and producing architecture without needing to build more, or without building so much. The pavilion's galleries were apparently empty—available space—while the models' bases floated beneath the ceiling, and were visible from the mezzanine. Few people would believe that Holland could have so many empty buildings, given the country's particularly high population density in a relatively small territory, much of it reclaimed from the sea. And yet millions of square meters of available space exist, without being paid for or used by anyone. By applying more flexible regulations, those spaces could be recycled for new uses and potentially for social housing. In fact, beyond Bouman's exposé of the situation in Holland, never in the history of humankind have there been so many potentially recyclable buildings.

Some architects have shown the way forward in this area by ingeniously recycling obsolete buildings—whether industrial, religious, or residential—and giving them a new lease of life. Contemporary social housing in former warehouses in London, in Barcelona's textile factories, or in Vienna's Gasometer buildings, are all good examples of adaptability to domestic programs. Perhaps most notably, Lacaton & Vassal have applied a strategy of remodeling social housing to improve buildings' quality and to add more essential features. "Essentiality is not the same as necessity. For example, more space in a residential unit is not exactly a need, but something that can be added. Therefore, essentiality and luxury are not synonymous, but one follows on from the other."[30] Anne Lacaton, working alongside her partner Jean-Philippe Vassal, together with Frédéric Druot and Christophe Hutin, created the Grand Parc housing estate in Bordeaux, winner of the 2019 Mies van der Rohe prize. The project was a transformation of three large blocks with 530 units, built in the 1960s. No one had to move out during the renovation work, and the aim was to make the units more sustainable and energy efficient, as well as more luminous, spacious, and accessible, while honoring the developer's pledge not to increase rents. "The intervention, which modifies three of the linear blocks providing social housing, refrains from interfering with the buildings' original structures.

30 Anne Lacaton, conference at the Universidad Diego Portales. Santiago de Chile, March 18, 2016.

Lacaton & Vassal Architectes, Frédéric Druot Architecture and Christophe Hutin Architecture. Transformation of 530 residential units - Grand Parc Bordeaux. Bordeaux, France, 2016. Before and after transformation.

Transformation of 530 residential units – Grand Parc Bordeaux. Before and after.

The philosophy of preserving all exploitable features of the constructions in question relates to a certain commitment to sustainability, but it also facilitates adapting an ambitious project to a limited budget. In this manner, through two simultaneous operations—extensions and additions—the useful floor area of each apartment increases with a screen of usable garden balconies, which gives every home a private, south-facing outside space. The arrangement of these winter gardens improves the thermal performance of the enclosure of the blocks, as does the quality of the materials introduced in the process and the insulation of the rear façades. The three-meter-deep exterior terraces that create the façades' new image are ample enough to create useful and comfortable spaces in the refurbished units."[31] This proposal aligns good design with social responsibility, developed with a modest budget and prioritizing transformation and reuse instead of demolition. This project shows that good architecture is not necessarily about new constructions, with iconic designs and large budgets, but that now, more than ever, recycling makes more sense.

31 *Arquitectura Viva*, no. 202. Project description.

Transformation of 530 residential units - Grand Parc Bordeaux.
Winter garden attached to existing façade of apartment 02.

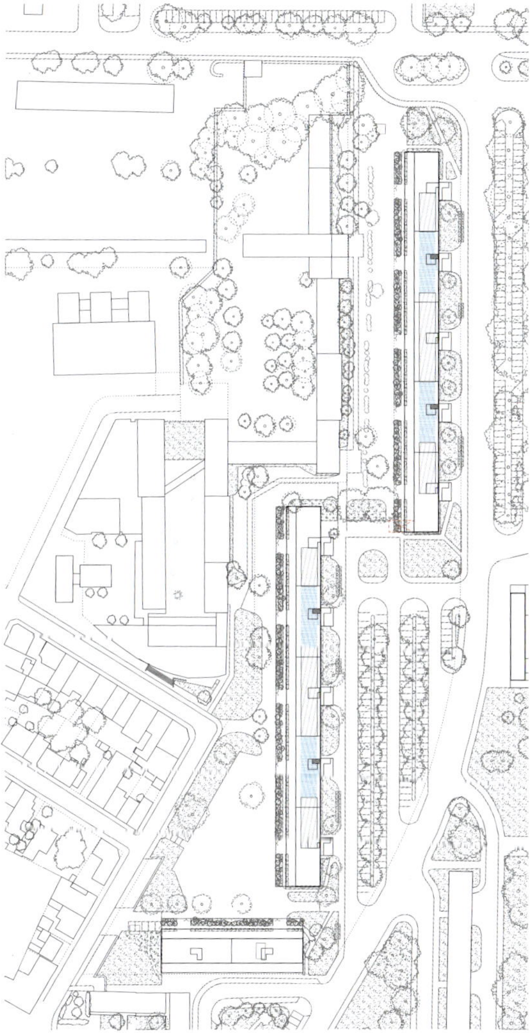

Site plan.

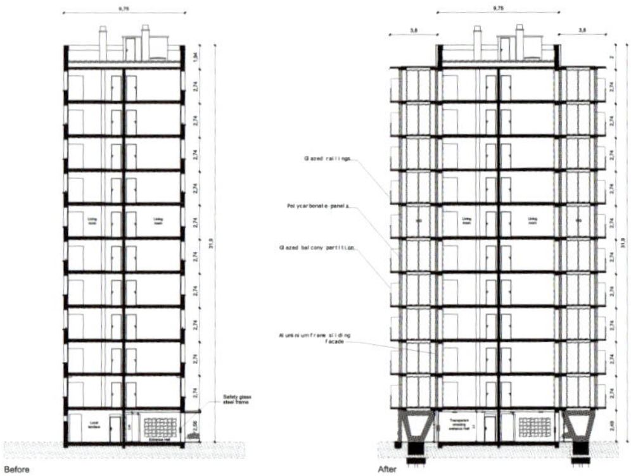

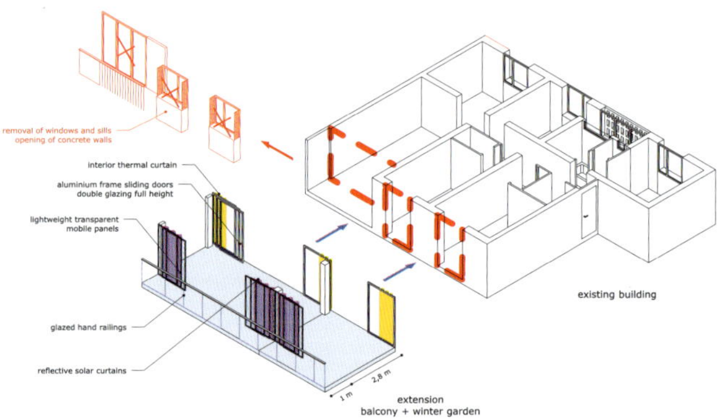

Transformation of 530 residential units - Grand Parc Bordeaux. Section of Building H before and after transformation; layout at start of extension.

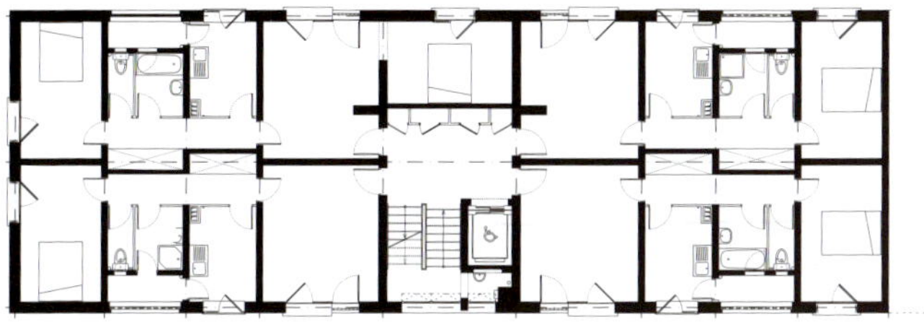

Before

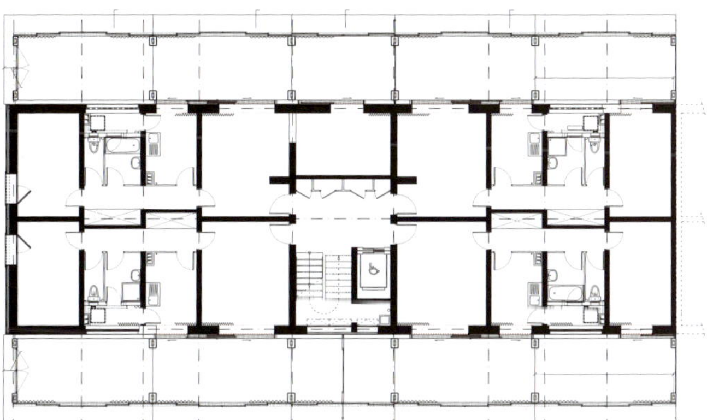

After

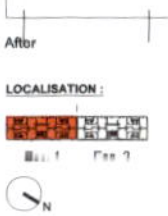

Floor plans of Building H before and after transformation.

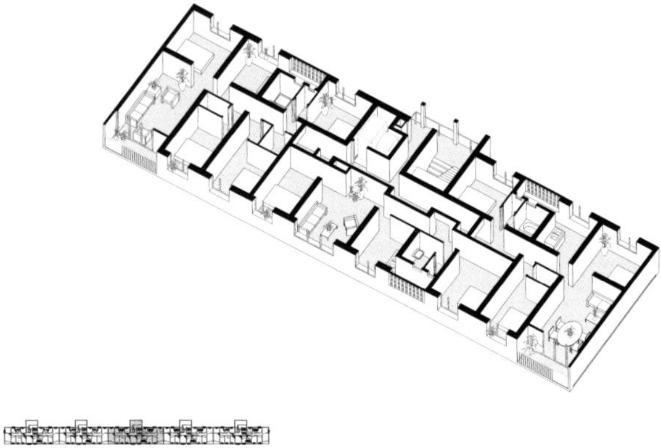

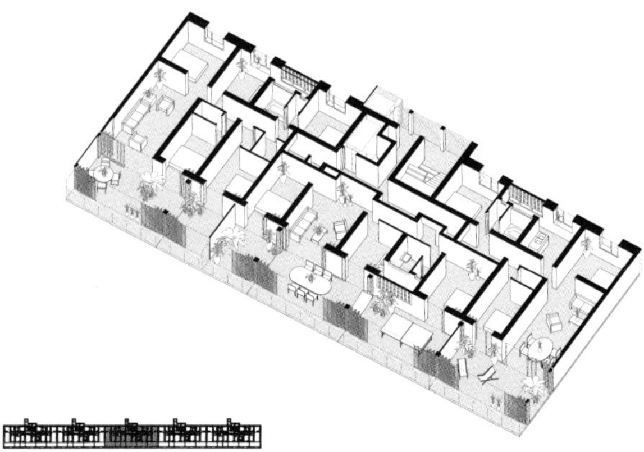

Transformation of 530 residential units - Grand Parc Bordeaux.
Axonometric diagrams: before and after the renovation.

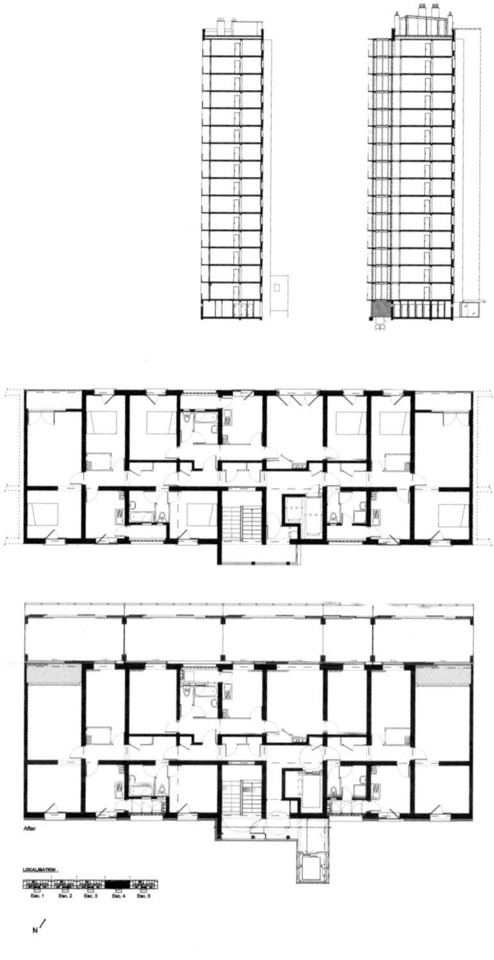

Floor plans and sections of Building G: before and after the renovation.

3. Key concepts

From each case study we can extract the essence that enabled a paradigm shift in the approach to social housing. Although a stock of ideas and proposals needs to be **replicable** on a large scale, these models shed light on some constant aspects of contemporary projects. A clear consensus exists on the need to **densify** our cities—from increasing the efficiency of infrastructures and transport, to adding value and creating a sense of community. We also need **typological diversity** to improve living conditions, whether through the (formal and informal) interaction of **strategies inherent in self-built housing** or **transformability** (expandible housing units) of domestic spaces.

This research takes stock of 20th-century ideas following the Modern movement's studies on mass-produced housing; it also refers to examples of social housing developments since Le Corbusier's Unité d'Habitation that have been developed around the world, particularly in Mexico and the rest of Latin America, with a new twist in recent years. Another focus is on examples of **community and cooperative self-management** from the previous century in Latin America, culminating in ELEMENTAL's proposals in Chile. We identify possible solutions in concepts that provide knowledge based on traditional and local techniques, provided they are replicable. And finally, sustainable strategies include **recycling** as a means of taking advantage of the potential of pre-existing buildings and recognizing their heritage value.

The projects are shown as alternatives for a market that continues replicating obsolete models of social housing projects that shun architects. They should be seen as a remedy for the sprawling growth of self-built housing in so many peripheral areas, with the resulting lack of urban infrastructure and the dangers of unsound constructions built on unsuitable land (ravines, garbage disposal sites, etc.). The inadequate offer of social housing often lies in the lack of **coordination** between public policies, developers, and citizens; architects are in a position and possess the knowledge to combine all the stakeholders' interests, increasing certainty and building, through social housing, better cities. Enrique Ciriani observed that "good architecture is just architecture, but good social housing creates cities."[1] At its core, this research offers strategic solutions, considering that both the earthquakes

1 Interview with Enrique Ciriani in Lima, October 2018.

and the recent pandemic revealed a need for large-scale solutions. Whatever helps mitigate the serious social housing problem in Mexico will be replicable around the world.

Image credits

1: Miquel Adrià and Alejandro Polo.

12–13: Published in *Le Corbusier, Les Trois établissements humains*, p. 35. FLC / ADAGP, Paris [2023] - Photography: FLC / ADAGP Images / SOMAAP / Mexico City / 2023.

24 TOP: © 2023. The Mies van der Rohe Archive. Digital image, The Museum of Modern Art, New York / Scala, Florence.

24 BOTTOM: Arquine.

27: Thomas Elsaesser, "The Architectural Postcard: Photography, Cinema, and Modernist Mass Media," *Grey Room*, 70 (Winter 2018), pp. 80–101. © 2018 by Grey Room, Inc. and the Massachusetts Institute of Technology. (grey_a_00232). Double page (p. 80).

28 TOP: © 2023. Digital image, The Museum of Modern Art, New York / Scala, Florence.

28 BOTTOM: © 2023. Digital image, The Museum of Modern Art, New York / Scala, Florence.

30–31: Betina Rincón.

32 TOP: Ernst May. Römerstadt.

32 BOTTOM: Reprography of *60 Jahre Aktienbaugesellschaft für kleine Wohnungen Frankfurt am Main 1890-1950*, Frankfurt am Main, 1950, p. 68.

33: Image from the magazine *Das Neue Frankfurt*, no. 5 (1926–1927). "Creative Commons / Frankfurter Küche

(Margarete Schütte-Lihotzky)" by Magadan reproduced under a CC-PD-Mark license.

34 TOP: ÖNB / Vienna 116.926-B.

34 BOTTOM: Reprography of *Narkomfin House and its Significance*, Narkomfin Foundation, Moscow, 2008, p. 58.

35: Photograph: C. Kramer. Canadian Centre for Architecture.

36: D. R. © Walter Gropius / VG Bild-Kunst / SOMAAP / Mexico / 2023.

37: "Creative Commons / Wohnstadt Carl Legien" from Architectuul under license CC BY-SA 3.0.

38: SOMAAP / Mexico City / 2023.

40 TOP: Shadrach Woods architectural records and papers, 1923–2008, Avery Architectural & Fine Arts Library, Columbia University.

40 BOTTOM: Alison and Peter Smithson. Robin Hood Gardens.

43: FLC / ADAGP, Paris [2023] - Photographs: FLC / ADAGP Images / SOMAAP / Mexico City / 2023.

44–45: Betina Rincón.

46, 47: FLC / ADAGP, Paris [2023] - Photographs: FLC / ADAGP Images / SOMAAP / Mexico City / 2023.

48: "Creative Commons / Unité d'Habitation 1" from michiel1972 under license CC-BY-SA-4.0.

49 TOP: "Creative Commons / Cité radieuse façade détail" by Pablosievert reproduced under license CC-BY-SA-4.0.

49 BOTTOM: "Creative Commons / Marseille - Cité Radieuse (16236331997)" by Fred Romero under license CC-BY-SA-4.0.

50: Photograms from the documentary *Teodoro en Concreto.* (2017). Directed by Emilio Maille. Script by Miquel Adrià. Mexico City, Arquine / El Caimán / El Canal 22 / El Colegio Nacional.

51: "Creative Commons / Cité radieuse (Marseille) de Le Corbusier, intérieur" by Michel-Georges Bernard under license CC-BY-SA-4.0.

52: Photograms from the documentary *Teodoro en Concreto.* (2017). Directed by Emilio Maille. Script by Miquel Adrià. Mexico City, Arquine / El Caimán / El Canal 22 / El Colegio Nacional.

53: "Creative Commons / Marseille - Cité Radieuse (16419384971)" by Fred Romero under license CC-BY-SA-4.0.

54 TOP: Public domain / Arquivo Nacional.

54 BOTTOM: Aerial view of Urbanización 2 de Diciembre (currently Urbanización 23 de Enero), Caracas, Venezuela, circa 1956 | Unknown author © Archivo Fotografía Urbana (Código 000431).

55 TOP: "Edificio Multifamiliar Miguel Alemán", 1949, Fondo Aerofotográfico Oblicuas, FAO_01_006174, Acervo Histórico Fundación ICA.

55 BOTTOM: Silvio Cavalcante. Reprography of *Latin America in Construction (1955–1980),* MoMA, New York, 2015, p. 139.

56: Arquine.

66-67: Reprography of *¡El tiempo construye!: el Proyecto Experimental de Vivienda (PREVI) de Lima: génesis y desenlace,* Editorial GG, Barcelona, 2008, p. 14.

68: Reprography of *¡El tiempo construye!: el Proyecto Experimental de Vivienda (PREVI) de Lima: génesis y desenlace,* Editorial GG, Barcelona, 2008, pp. 16, 17.

69: Reprography of *¡El tiempo construye!: el Proyecto Experimental de Vivienda (PREVI) de Lima: génesis y desenlace,* Editorial GG, Barcelona, 2008.

70 TOP: © Peter Land.

70 BOTTOM: Reprography of *¡El tiempo construye!: el Proyecto Experimental de Vivienda (PREVI) de Lima: génesis y desenlace,* Editorial GG, Barcelona, 2008, p. 70.

71: Arquine.

72, 73: Reprography of *CAPBA* (journal of Colegio de Arquitectos de la Provincia de Buenos Aires), no. 22, 2017, p. 64.

74: Reprography of *Tlatelolco. Un concepto de ciudad,* Arquine, Mexico City, 2020, p. 141.

77, 78: Oscar Hagerman.

81, 83–85: Carlos González Lobo.

86: ELEMENTAL.

89 TOP: Photographs: Tadeuz Jalocha. Courtesy of ELEMENTAL.

89 BOTTOM, 92, 93: ELEMENTAL.

94 TOP: Filippo Poli.

94 BOTTOM: FLC / ADAGP, Paris [2023] - Photographs: FLC / ADAGP Images / SOMAAP / Mexico City / 2023.

95: Filippo Poli.

96–101: ELEMENTAL.

102, 105: JC Arquitectura / Juan Carral.

106: Victor Ebergenyi.

108–111: César Béjar. Courtesy of JC Arquitectura / Juan Carral.

112: Reprography of *Redensificación urbana,* Infonavit + Arquine, Mexico City, 2018, pp. 46–47.

114–115: Reprography of *Redensificación urbana,* Infonavit + Arquine, Mexico City, 2018, pp. 116–119.

116–117: Reprography of *Redensificación urbana,* Infonavit + Arquine, Mexico City, 2018, pp. 175–179.

118–119: Reprography of *Redensificación urbana,* Infonavit + Arquine, Mexico City, 2018, pp. 79–83.

120–121: Reprography of *Redensificación urbana,* Infonavit + Arquine, Mexico City, 2018, pp. 229–233.

123: TAX. Alberto Kalach.

124–125: Photographs: Jaime Navarro. Courtesy of TAX. Alberto Kalach.

126–127: TAX. Alberto Kalach.

128, 131, 132, 134, 136–143: Manuel Gausa, Actar Arquitectura.

144: ENORME Studio.

145: Photographs: Javier de Paz García. Courtesy of ENORME Studio.

146: ENORME Studio.

147: Photographs: Javier de Paz García. Courtesy of ENORME Studio.

148: OFFPOLINN.

149: Photographs: Miguel de Guzmán. Courtesy of OFFPOLINN.

150: Reprography of *Archi & BD, la ville dessinée,* Cité d'Architecture & du patrimoine, Paris, 2010, p. 115.

153: Reprography of *Archi & BD, la ville dessinée,* Cité d'Architecture & du patrimoine, Paris, 2010, p. 215.

154, 155: Nobuaki Nakagawa.

156, 157: Kazuyo Sejima & Associates.

158–159: Betina Rincón.

161: Photographs: Iwan Baan.

162, 164, 165: OMA / Ole Scheeren.

167: Photographs: Iwan Baan.

168, 169: BIG.

170: Miquel Adrià.

173, 174, 176: Photographs: Philippe Ruault. Courtesy of Lacaton & Vassal Architectes.

177–181: Lacaton & Vassal Architectes.

Bios

Alejandro Aravena graduated as an architect from the Universidad Pontificia de Chile and completed postgraduate studies at IUAV and Accademia di Belle Arti di Venezia. In 2001 he founded ELEMENTAL. Pritzker Prize Laureate in 2016 and is currently jury chair.

Andrea Griborio graduated as an architect from the Universidad de Zulia (Venezuela), with a master's from UPC (Barcelona). Executive Director of MEXTRÓPOLI Architecture and City Festival and professor of the Master's in Housing at CENTRO.

Miquel Adrià graduated as an architect from the Escola Tècnica Superior d'Arquitectura de Barcelona with a PhD in Architecture from the Universidad Europea de Madrid. Director of Arquine MEXTRÓPOLI Architecture and City Festival. Director of the Architecture School at CENTRO.

Housing: Strategies for Urban Redensification was printed and bound in January 2024 by Offset Rebosán in Mexico City. It was set in typefaces of the Sofia Pro family. Printed in C1S cardboard and 115 g couché paper.